The Voyage of Dollier de Casson & Galinée 1669-1670

The Voyage of Dollier de Casson & Galinée 1669-1670

THIS PARADISE OF CANADA

John D. Ayre

I leave to you to imagine whether we suffered in the midst of this abundance in the earthly paradise of Canada; I call it so, because there is assuredly no more beautiful region.

From the Journal of René Bréhant de Galinée, 1670

Ton histoire est une épopée des plus brillants exploits.
Your history is an epic of the most shining achievements.

From the National Anthem of Canada

Dedication

To my wife Susie,
" L'architecte de ma félicité "
and
to my Grandchildren,
"May you always be possessed of the spirit of adventure."

Contents

Acknowledgments · xi
Introduction · xiii

Chapter 1   Historical Background · 1
Henri's Story   *Commencement* · 7
Chapter 2   Genesis and Dollier de Casson · 9
Henri's Story   *L'Arrivée* · 18
Chapter 3   Galinée and La Salle · 20
Henri's Story   *Préparations* · 22
Chapter 4   Departure & Ascent of the St. Lawrence · 23
Henri's Story   *Mon Travail* · 28
Chapter 5   Canoes and Paddlers · 29
Chapter 6   Iroquois and Northern New York · 34
Henri's Story   *Village des Iroquois* · 41
Chapter 7   Head of the Lake and Jolliet · 42
Henri's Story   *Pays d'en Haut* · 45
Chapter 8   Tinaoutoua and Descent of the Grand River · · · · · · · · · · · · · · · · · 47
Henri's Story   *Seul* · 51
Chapter 9   The Over Wintering of 1669 - 1670 At Port Dover · · · · · · · · · · · · 52
Henri's Story   *L'Hivernement* · 56
Chapter 10   Food and Provisions · 57
Chapter 11   Exodus: Spring 1670 · 61
Henri's Story   *Le Temps de misère* · 69
Chapter 12   Disaster at Point Pelée · 70
Henri's Story   *Vers le Sault* · 75
Chapter 13   Sault Ste. Marie and Return to Montréal · · · · · · · · · · · · · · · · · · · 76
Henri's Story   *Chez-nous* · 80
Chapter 14   Revelations, the Journal & the Map · 81
Chapter 15   Dénouement · 85
Chapter 16   Conclusion · 91
Henri's Story   *Mes Rêves* · 93
Chapter 17   The Untold Story · 94

End Notes to Chapters · 95
Appendix A Location of the Wintering Site at Port Dover · · · · · · · · · · · · 103
Appendix B Chronology of the Voyage · 107
Illustrations · 111
Bibliography · 113
Index · 119
About the Author · 121

Acknowledgments

———

I AM GRATEFUL FOR THE assistance of the Norfolk Historical Society at Simcoe, Ontario in researching this book. It was James Coyne, a member of the N.H.S who over a century ago last wrote at length of Dollier and Galinée. I am also grateful to the staff of the Norfolk Public Library who accommodated my many requests for inter-library loans of obscure books and those long out of print.

The Law Society of Upper Canada provided me with information concerning James Coyne.

I received some very helpful input from Eric Fernberg, Collections Specialist, Arms and Technology of the Canadian War Museum in Ottawa concerning the firearms our adventurers would have used.

I also wish to thank the Society of Saint-Sulpice *Compagnie des Prêtres de Saint-Sulpice* in Montréal, Paris and Rome of whom I made inquiries concerning Galinée and from whom I received prompt and encouraging replies with the information they had available.

Above all, my wife Susan to whom this book is dedicated showed great patience when I vanished into my home office to work on what I called "the Project". This Project is complete.

Introduction

THREE HUNDRED AND FIFTY YEARS ago, two French priests of the Order of Saint Sulpice, accompanied by seven soldiers, set off from Montréal in three birch bark canoes on a voyage of over three thousand kilometres.

They would suffer near starvation and experience vicious weather. They would spend five months wintering in the forest fearful of expected Iroquois attack. Yet through all this and much more they would survive.

We know of these things because one of the priests kept a journal and drew a map. Nonetheless, the narrative of their journey to the interior of Canada, undertaken in the year 1669 by the Sulpician priests Francois Dollier de Casson and René de Bréhant de Galinée, along with their seven companions, is a little known story that deserves a better understanding. It is a tale that includes many sub-plots and themes. It includes soldiers, priests, European Royalty and First Nations. It touches on the story of European dynastic desires and mother nature's resistance to intruders. It is a story of courage, resolve, deceit and despair. Even cannibalism surfaces in the narrative!

The events described herein occurred almost three and a half centuries before the date of this writing. The complete and utter faith in the Catholic Church and the Sulpician Order possessed by the principal protagonists Dollier and Galinée will be contrasted with the occasional deceit and motives of a parallel player in the saga, René-Robert Cavelier Sieur de La Salle.

When I first heard of the journey of Dollier and Galinée I wondered who they were, what they had seen and done and what it must have been like for Europeans to travel by birch bark canoe through the wilderness that was Canada in the years 1669 and 1670. Upon reading the text of the Journal written by Galinée and studying the map that he drew, I knew there existed a window into the past that could be opened that would answer my questions and that might also interest others. The original of Galinée's Journal, is twenty-four sheets of paper long, neatly written on both sides for a total of forty-eight pages. Along with some other related documents it is archived in the National Library of France. Dollier too would write his own Journal but declared that having read Galinée's he considered it superior to his own which he then destroyed. This loss to history does serve to some extent as a circumstantial declaration by Dollier of the accuracy of what Galinée wrote.

The earliest reproduction of Galinée's Journal was not published until 1866 by Etienne Faillon in his work "*Histoire de la Colonie Francaise en Canada*." Faillon had access to other original and near contemporary sources some of which are now lost.

The Frenchman Pierre Margry who was the Director of the Archives of the Marine and Colonies also wrote on the subject in the middle of the Nineteenth Century. His work *Découvertes et Établissements* is available and I was able to make some use of it. Somewhat surprisingly I found that the only detailed, dedicated and scholarly article written in English on the topic appeared over one hundred years ago in 1903 in the Ontario Historical Journal authored by James H Coyne. **1**

Coyne was a lawyer and at one time the President of the Ontario Historical Society. He was a prolific writer of early Ontario History and took a particular interest in the voyage of Dollier and Galinée. His publication in 1903 and continued interest ultimately led to the identification of Dollier's Wintering Site in Port Dover, Ontario and its designation in 1919 as a National Historic Site. I was able to copy the map Coyne included in that long out of date publication and to use the many annotations made by Galinée that appeared on the map as a cross reference to the text of the Journal the latter kept.

I will not pretend to approach the style that James Coyne presented in his 1903 article rather I choose to bring my own approach to bear in an attempt to reach a wider Twenty-First Century audience. After all, this is an adventure story. The names of persons intimately involved leap off the pages of Canadian and American history, such as René Robert Cavelier Sieur de La Salle, Adrien Jolliet, Intendant Jean Talon and Jean Baptiste Colbert, Senior Minister of France. Even the Roi-Soleil himself, the most powerful man in Europe, King Louis XIV makes an occasional appearance on these pages.

Some of those who participated in the voyage were motivated by a burning desire to save souls, others were motivated by money. In the end result discoveries were made and recorded in Galinée's Journal and on his map that would expand the knowledge of Europeans of the interior of what would one day be known as Southern Ontario.

Concerning the Native tribes, the Ottawas and Potawatomis and above all the Iroquois, Galinée wrote about each one of them. As our principal recorder, Galinée even reveals the existence of a mysterious First Nations slave, pivotal to this story and an equally mysterious and somewhat devious Dutch interpreter.

I also ventured to access some near contemporary accounts as adjuncts to the Galinée text such as the Journal written by Louis-Armand Baron Lahontan in 1703 or even the much later Journal of Alexander McKenzie written in the late 18th Century because as chroniclers who partially travelled across the same landscapes as our adventurers they can materially add to some of the descriptions of places or portages that Galinée wrote about. I also studied texts written by Samuel de Champlain in the early 1600's. Champlain wrote detailed accounts and published extensively on the subject of his travels.

The core of the story I have written about comes however from Galinée's Journal and his commentaries written on the map he drew at the completion of the journey in the summer of 1670.

Ideally this work will appeal to those with an interest in Canadian history, the history of First Nations as well as to students of geography. History and historical narratives rarely speak to only one audience and if this book appeals to the readers senses on any of those alternate fronts it will have been worth the effort. The reader will quickly find that in this story, geography and weather determined the narrative as much as the people did.

The text has two components. The first and major part of each Chapter is the historical non-fictional account of the voyage of Dollier and Galinée. The second component found at the end of most Chapters are the writings of the fictional "*Henri.*" Henri is my creation and represents a character whose observations might have been made as one of the ex-soldiers who was on the journey. I am the voice of *Henri*, or rather, he is mine. He is my vehicle to speak to the reader and to convey a sense of what it was like for the men accompanying Dollier and Galinée. As a fictive character *Henri* hopefully will speak as if his voice is a time traveller that takes the reader back in time and lets the reader feel the pain of paddling all day, to feel the sting of swarms of mosquitos and to sense what it was like to be alone in the forest or on the choppy waters of the Great Lakes.

I have attempted to use the French spelling as it appears in Galinée's Journal. This will explain to the modern French speaker the absence of accents and the use of some archaic tenses and words. If Galinée used an accent then so too did this writer. If he did not then neither did I. Unless otherwise sourced if a sentence in the text is *Italicized* the reader can assume it comes from Galinée's Journal.

Chapter Seventeen is a final short fictional commentary that relates part of the story through native eyes. I entitled it "The Untold Story." I acknowledge my European/Canadian heritage fully and the inherent euro-centric bias that must creep into my analysis. However as I read and re-read the text of Galinée's Journal I recognized that there was an alternate point of view from which the story could be told, through the eyes of the First Nations.

I have no doubt that I will have imperfectly told that story because of my non Native roots but as the Seneca leader and Prophet Sganyodaiyo (also known as *Handsome Lake*) once observed *"we are all Natives of the earth"* and if I succeed in making the reader aware of the other possible First Nations viewpoint then I will have achieved one of my goals.

It is with some care and respect that I refer to the Natives of the story, the tribes of the Ottawas, Nipissings, Seneca et cetera, either by those names or as "Natives" and on rare occasion as "Indians" but only where the term is used by one of the historical characters. The latter term is clearly out of favour in common language although I note the Federal Government of Canada still administers the Department of "Indian" Affairs. Frequently in my travels I pass the Six Nations of the Grand River Territory whose Band Council have a sign directing motorists onto the "Six Nations Indian Reserve."

When the fictional narrator *"Henri"* speaks as a former soldier of the seventeenth century he uses the term "Indian."

Hopefully my sensitivity to the nomenclature will be apparent throughout. I do observe that the language used by Galinée to describe the Natives was often harsh. It will also be one of the themes of this book that whatever the relationship was between the French travellers and the Natives, the French could never have ventured forward on their journey or arrived back home alive without the constant assistance in one form or another of the "Indians."

With respect to place names I have used modern names for the modern reader. Port Dover Ontario was not called Port Dover in 1669. Galinée simply called it, *"the place where we overwintered."* Among the Europeans it had no name, nor did Port Stanley, or the future settlement on the straits later named by the French simply as "the narrows or, Détroit." Ville Marie or Montréal as we call it today was alternately called by both of those names in 1669 although the former usage was more frequently used by religious orders. Some geographic features such as Lake Erie had names given them by the Natives or from verbal descriptions given by earlier explorers. Other places that we know today by their French names, like Point Pelée (from the fact that the Peninsula was bare or peeled of trees) would receive their names after our travellers had passed by.

Calendar dates referred to in the text correspond to our current calendar as by the 17th Century the French had been using the modern calendar given to the world by Pope Gregory XIII in 1582, while the British struggled on with the Julian calendar until finally adopting the Gregorian model in the middle of the 18th Century.

In an earlier part of my life I was a Crown Attorney in Ontario arguing criminal cases in Court based on the results of police investigations as recorded in what was called "the Crown Brief." Some Crown Briefs were long and detailed, others less so. Some possessed details simple to comprehend and to convey to the Court while others were extremely complicated. I sought to develop the skill to assist Judges and Juries in determining the truth of what occurred in a given case by going beyond what the written witness statements recorded. As a lawyer I sought to pierce the sterile words of the file and connect the themes of the Crown brief to convey what actually happened and what it was like as events unfolded.

In this book I attempt to do something similar using Galinée's text and his map as my "Brief "and to give the reader a sense of the realities that Dollier and his companions experienced. This book is my attempt to reconstruct the experience of Dollier and Galinée's journey and their seven companions three and a half centuries after it occurred. I want to take the reader on a journey into the past.

Using Galinée's Journal as though it were a Crown Brief, I looked for those themes that were internally consistent with known facts and those that were not. I examined assertions for internal consistency within the Journal and the heavily annotated map with known external consistencies taken from secondary or near contemporary sources. In that process my goal has been to relate principally by the text and also via the fictional, but accurate story as told by *Henri*….what the experience was actually like for these men as they travelled into the unknown.

As to whether I have succeeded or not in achieving my goals, the reader will be my jury.

The year was 1669. The narrative of the exploits of the Voyage of Dollier and Galinée is part of the epic of Canadian history.

It is time to retell their story.

CHAPTER 1
Historical Background

THE PRINCIPAL STORY OF THE Voyage of Dollier and Galinée begins in the year 1669 with another story, one told by a man who was a slave. His story resonated with the persons he told it to and they believed him. The slave was male and was a member of a band of Natives from the south west in what we would now call the Ohio country. What is also known about him is that he had been captured by another First Nations Tribe and ultimately found himself among the Nipissing (called by the French "*Nepissiriniens*"). He was a captive amongst the Algonkian speaking people who lived in the Region of the lake that bears their name, near present day North Bay, Ontario.

Slavery had existed for time immemorial amongst the First Nations of North America. **1** In the seventeenth century it was nothing like the full scale industrial and racialized slavery that black people of Africa suffered at the hands of Europeans and others, but it was slavery nonetheless.

Slavery was practiced by both the Algonkian tribes and the Iroquois as spoils of war. Slaves might be kept for years only to be exchanged for a tribe's own members who had been taken captive. Sometimes slaves were ritually tortured and killed. On occasion slaves were simply adopted and absorbed into the tribe to replenish tribal numbers depleted from disease, starvation and conflict. Most of the time slaves dreamt of survival and possible return home. Some escaped.

In 1669, one particular slave, held by the Nipissing Chief Nitarikyk, (Galinée calls Nitarikyk a "*capitaine*." The word "leader" is a sufficient intepretation) had a story to tell. He must have been a person who was very perceptive and astute. Late in the previous year of 1668, a French priest of the Order of Saint Sulpice named Francois Dollier de Casson had travelled to live among the Nipissing in order to learn their language in the hopes of being better able to proselytize the Catholic faith and spread the Gospel. **2** Thus the slave would have first encountered Dollier. The spreading of Christianity was one, but only one of the chief aims of the French presence and French plans for their nascent colony of New France. Dollier had only arrived in Canada three years previously.

This slave "with no name" had been sent by his master (no doubt not alone) to Montréal where he related to Dollier's Superior, the Abbé Gabriel de Queylus, a story that he was a member of a remote tribe, living some seven or eight hundred leagues from Montréal in a land that was thickly populated and that his tribe might prove fruitful ground in the Priest's quest for the salvation of souls. **3** Dollier's Superior listened and wrote a letter to Dollier who was still in the Nipissing territory and then entrusted the same slave to deliver the return letter to him, a task subsequently completed by this nameless letter carrier. Upon receipt of the letter, Dollier immediately embraced the idea and the concept for the journey was born.

Thus it came to pass that later that year of 1669, Francois Dollier de Casson a Priest of the Society of Saint Sulpice, left Ville-Marie (Montréal) accompanied by a Deacon of his Order, René Bréhant de Galinée and seven soldiers recruited for the journey from the garrison. They would leave on a voyage into lands that were untraveled by Europeans. Their precise destination was unknown to them. The date of return was equally unknown. The route to be taken was uncertain. Their collective ability to survive a complete winter in the wilderness was untested.

What was known to them was their precise purpose. They were going to the lands in the south west as described by the slave, to the Ohio country and there they would spread the Gospel and save souls. Their zeal for this goal would take them where no European had left a recorded trail. They were willing to test their resolve and inner strength to the fullest to achieve that purpose. As circumstances would demonstrate they would need both to in order to survive.

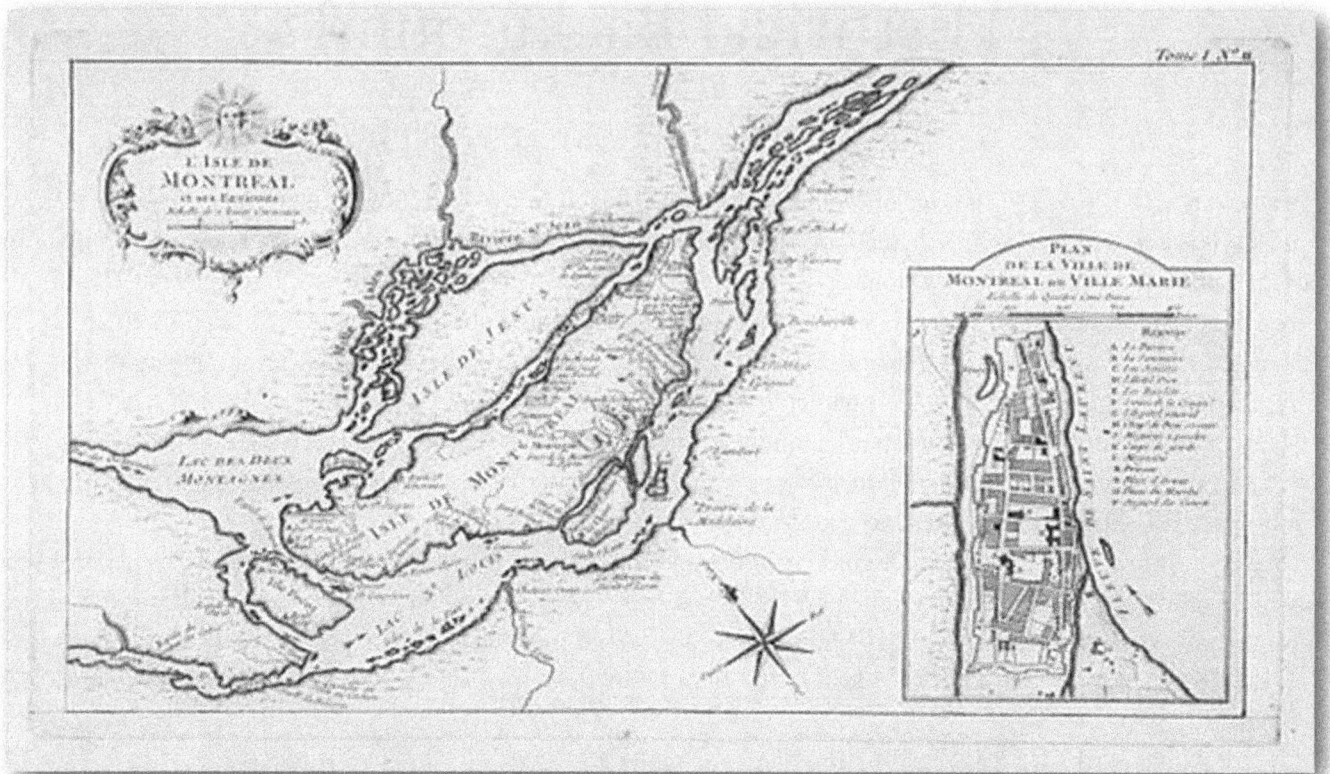

Figure.1 An early map of Montréal from the late Seventeenth Century.

Dollier, Galinée and their companions put their paddles into the waters and set off in three fragile canoes for a voyage that would last almost one year and cover several thousands of kilometers into lands and waters whose hazards were many.

France was experiencing a religious revival of conservative Catholicism. The Thirty Years War (1618-1648) that had torn Europe apart at the cost of millions of lives had ended but had not extinguished the zeal of the clergy. "Zeal" was in fact a word that would appear frequently in writings of the era, including Galinée's. One was either possessed of "zeal" or *zèle* in the service of the King and the Church or one was consigned to political impotence if suspected or accused of having a lack of zeal. It was a word that was often over-used but whose significance was not lost on any in France or her colony of New France. The Edict of Nantes of 1598 provided a degree of toleration to Protestants (it would be revoked in 1685) but that policy of toleration by the State had virtually no application in New France. Protestantism or the *"Religion Prétendue Reformée"* as it was referred to in France had little place in New France and as it grew the colony would be deeply Catholic. The Jesuits, Récollets and Sulpicians would ensure this fact. 4

Francois Dollier de Casson was a man who was possessed of much zeal,*"un zèle fort "*Galinée would call it… zeal for his Church and for his calling. A more modern term might be "passion" but either term explains his resolve to carry out the mission to the unknown peoples of the distant southwest, of whose existence the French had been informed by the slave held by the Nipissing.

Figure: 2 Champlain. Self-portrait from his drawing of 1613 depicting his earlier encounter with the Iroquois. When he fired his arquebus he killed at least one Iroquois and wounded several others as the weapon was quadruple-shotted.

There were some Iroquois living on the north shore of Lake Ontario both at the site of the future City of Toronto on the Humber River and elsewhere including one location in particular that Galinée wrote about, near modern day Hamilton. This latter group are sometimes described as the North Shore Iroquois. This label in no way diminishes their kinship with all other Iroquois or their war-making abilities.

What was it then that led to the continuation of an Iroquois and French conflict? It came down to trade. Because of their unique geographic position on the continent, the Iroquois in general and the Mohawk in particular controlled access to the interior of the continent. Any tribe to the west that wanted to trade with the French or the Dutch at New York or Fort Orange (Albany) had to go through them. The English were still very much hemmed in by the Appalachian chain of mountains that would not be penetrated by the Europeans for years to come. **6**

The Iroquois controlled access onto the St. Lawrence River by virtue of their homeland. From the Atlantic coast at what would be New York City one could travel up the Hudson River for a considerable distance in a large vessel. Indeed this is just what the ill-fated Henry Hudson had done in 1609 in his ship the *"Half Moon."* At the point where the river became too shallow for large craft the Dutch built their trading post, Fort Orange.

However this was the northernmost Dutch post on the Hudson River because the Iroquois who lived in the lands between Fort Orange and the Hudson River westward to Lake Ontario wanted no Europeans there. In their desire to control and monopolize the trade between Europeans and all other tribes to the north and the west the Iroquois were prepared to fight and die. With The Iroquois sitting at the junction of the great water routes, the St Lawrence, the Hudson and the Great Lakes no one could pass behind this "curtain" the Iroquois had drawn without the them knowing about it, facilitating it, or blocking it as it would impact on their economic interests.

The strength of that curtain is demonstrated by the fact that prior to the time of our narrative, French voyageurs and a few Priests such as the Jesuit Jean Nicollet had travelled by 1634 not only to the present location of Sault Ste. Marie but much further west, including Green Bay Michigan, la Baie des Puants. By 1661 Nicollet's fellow Jesuit René Ménard likely even penetrated as far as the Wisconsin River which ultimately flows into the Mississippi. Why was it that the French had been able to travel so far into the heart of North America only by the Ottawa-Nipissing route but not southward, not even once to Lake Erie? Simply put, until the recent cessation of hostilities the Iroquois would not allow it. Not even the Ottawa-Nipissing route was entirely safe for the French.

In the year 1660 a French colonist and fur trader named Adam Dollard had been in battle with a large group of Iroquois at the Long Sault Rapids on the Ottawa River. One theory is that he intercepted and delayed the advancing war party thus "saving Montréal." The other theory is that the Iroquois caught him poaching on what they saw as their turf. A battle followed with the Iroquois laying siege to the fortified stockade Dollard had hastily built, but in the fight that ensued Dollard and most of his group were killed. *"Jour de Dollard"* was celebrated until 2003 in Québec (currently celebrated as *Journée Nationale des Patriotes*).

It was evident to the Iroquois that their supply of beaver was limited and by 1669 had become severely depleted. The great inventory of furs lay with other tribes to the west and above all to the north where the furs were of a consistently better quality. The economics and political power that went with the trade were not misunderstood in the least by the Iroquois. They had to maintain control of the trade with the English/Dutch at Albany and the French at Québec as much as possible. Interlopers were not welcome. The French at Québec, Montréal and in Paris thought otherwise.

The Ottawas (from an Algonkian word meaning "trader") were far to the north. The Potawatomis were located to the south and west in the area of Michigan and Ohio and the Susquehannocks of Pennsylvania and the Chesapeake region were known to by the French as *Andastes* and of them we will hear more. The Susquehannocks had warred for years with the Iroquois and were engaged with their own conflicts with the English. The Iroquois, though weakened by recent events were supreme in the Region of the Great Lakes as amongst First Nations. The French did not perceive things quite this way.

Small as it was with barely six hundred inhabitants, Montréal became the focus of Iroquois attacks. Clearly it was meant to be a permanent French settlement and the Iroquois did not approve. In the years between 1660 and 1666 attacks on the town were nearly constant. The inhabitants had to farm in groups while armed and many were taken captive, some to be tortured and killed, others to be made slaves and some to be returned in exchange when the French took an Iroquois alive. The Iroquois orbit of power was very widely spread by the mid-Seventeenth Century.

Then came the morning in July 1669 when a group of men in their birch bark canoes paused momentarily. A prayer would have been said for their benefit from the shoreline of Ville-Marie, a small and imperiled settlement that would one day become the great city of Montréal. The two Sulpician priests each sat in their canoes no doubt pondering the distance they had travelled from the Cathedral of Saint Sulpice in Paris and their birthplaces in Brittany.

And then all that needed to be said had been said. The benediction had been given. The first paddle touched the water and all the men pulled together. With that first stroke of the paddle, the first of countless thousands of paddle strokes they moved silently into the waters of the St. Lawrence, turned westward and into the unknown. The story of the journey of Dollier and Galinée into the wilderness is not widely known in Canadian history and means the time has come that like them, we too should make a beginning.

Figure 3. Louis XIV. Painting of 1701 by Rigaud.
" *Le Roi le veut* " " The King wills it", was the policy of France and of New France.
Louis would be the longest reigning Sovereign of Canada from 1643 until his death in 1715.

HENRI'S STORY
Commencement

Je m'appelle Henri. My name is Henri. I was born in Blois. According to what my late parents told me when I was but a child I must now be in my 66th year. They named me after an earlier King of France who was kind to those who shared our beliefs. For we were Protestant Huguenots, and not of the Catholic faith although for my part that would change upon my arrival in New France at Québec as a soldier of the Carignan-Salières Regiment in the year '65 when I was but twenty years old. Upon our arrival in Québec we soldiers who were Huguenot were given the choice of converting to the Roman Church or returning immediately to France. I chose to abjure the protestant church after the difficult passage we had experienced in the ship but a few men refused and were put back on the ships.

Born as I was of a large family my only education came from what my wits enabled me to learn and from the inspiration given me by my younger sister Catherine, who alone among our family learned to read and write. She would join the same Blessed Order of Benedictine nuns Père Dollier's eldest sister. It was to her that I told this story and she who wrote it and read it back to me. It is the story of a voyage that took me to a place where the endless trees stood as though they were the stone columns of the grandest cathedrals of this Kingdom of France and the enormous lakes were like of a fresh water ocean and whose sounds and silences and whose greatness I shall never see again.

I am now an old man. I am dying. I sit on a bench in my home in Blois in this Year of our Lord 1711 and tell my sister my story so that she may record it. My revered sister is now the Superior of the Benedictine nuns whose care of sinners such as me shall render them into sainthood in the next life to come

I know my sister has faithfully recorded what I saw. And now by the words she has written and read back to me I shall tell it to you whoever you may be. Once I journeyed with others of my countrymen to the edges of the known world in small boats made of birch bark. I travelled in the great wilderness beyond New France called the Pays d'en Haut, to the Upper Country with Father Francois Dollier de Casson and his Deacon René Bréhant de Galinée.

I saw many wonderful things. This is what I saw.

CHAPTER 2

Genesis and Dollier de Casson

————

*"The Chief had a slave the Ottawa's had presented to him…who gave a description of the route to his country
that he made everybody believe he could easily conduct any persons that should wish to go there with him "*

JOURNAL OF GALINÉE

THE NIPISSING CHIEF NITARIKYK SENT the nameless slave to Montréal. Thus began the sequence of events that concerns us.

Upon arrival in Montréal the slave performed the task assigned to him but in a significant turn of fate, contrived or not, the slave who described himself as coming from a "remote" tribe in the southwest also had contact with Abbé de Queylus, the Superior of the Sulpicians in Montréal.

Founded in 1641 by Father Jean-Jacques Olier in Paris the Sulpician Order (named after the Seventh Century French Saint, Sulpitius the Pious) was focused principally on the training of clergy. Their home, the Cathedral of Saint Sulpice in Paris is second in size only to the more famous Cathedral of Notre Dame (Their history in Canada has recently been chronicled in *"Les Sulpiciens de Montréal. Une Histoire de pouvoir et discrétion. 1657-2007."* Deslandres, Dickinson, Hubert ed. Editions Fides 2007).

Born in France in 1612, Gabriel Thubières de Levy de Queylus had arrived in Canada in July 1657. He was well educated and had significant financial resources at his disposal. He was a co-founder of the Sulpician Seminary in Montréal. He had been recommended for the all-important post of Bishop of Québec but he was not acceptable to the Jesuits. The title of Bishop of Québec would ultimately go to Francois Laval. These appointments were a manifestation of a power struggle taking place at the French Court of Louis XIV between Church and State. Adherents of the Gallician Church supported appointments that were made with Louis' approval as opposed to the ultra-montane faction, of which the Jesuits can be included, who viewed such appointments as the pure preserve of Rome.

An accommodation of sorts was reached when de Queylus was named Vicar General of Montréal and the entire island of Montréal was placed under the charge of the Sulpicians in 1663. Founded in 1642 by Maisonneuve, the outpost of Ville-Marie was located on the Island of Montréal, which had been so named on maps for over one hundred years after being visited by Jacque Cartier in 1535. The name Ville Marie would fall out of common usage in the early 18th Century.

Figure 4. Warrior. Sketch circa 1700
Louis Nicolas. *Codex Canadensis.*

De Queylus believed the story told by the slave that he could lead the French to his homeland in the southwest in the territory later known as the Ohio and assist in his people's conversion and that there would be many people there who would be ready to accept the Gospels. It could not have really been surprising to anyone that the slave just might be willing to say he knew the way since any route took him away from his condition of slavery with the Nipissing!

The slave's tale so intrigued de Quelyus that he sent a return letter to Dollier in the same country from whence the slave had come. The slave thus returned back to the Nipissing Territory with the letter. One can imagine the day when, in the still frozen forests of the Nipissing Territory, the Sulpician Priest Dollier de Casson quietly read the letter from his Superior de Queylus.

As his name implies, Francois Dollier de Casson was born in 1636 in the Chateau at Casson-sur-l'Erdre in lower Britany, near the City of Nantes. The River Erdre flows into the Garonne and the Chateau in which Dollier was born still stands today as a private residence. His parents were of sound financial means and it may have been his father's military patrimony that led the young Dollier to serve the King as a cavalry officer in the French Army between 1653 and 1656. He was a young well educated man who had seen war firsthand. He would see war once again as a Priest when he came to Canada.

Holding the position of Cavalry Officer confirms that Dollier and his family had considerable financial resources since at that time Officers supplied their horses, equipment and servants at their own expense. No Officer was expected nor socially permitted to tend to his own horse nor would any Officer be possessed of only one mount. Dollier had money and this relative affluence would show itself in later years. After three years of military service he left the army. Leaving war behind, for the moment at least, Dollier made the decision to join the Society of Saint Sulpice.

After completing his studies, in due course Dollier was ordained a Priest. He was by then a man who had seen the world and knew its ways. He was among the best educated of Frenchmen. It may be that the reader perceives the description of him in this work as a "heroic" character, and the reader may judge this for themselves at the conclusion of this writing. Yet like all heroes, his human failings as perceived from the Twenty First Century will also emerge in what follows.

Anxious to work in the New World on behalf of his Order he sought permission to travel to New France and although initially passed over in favour of others, he was eventually selected to go. One direct source for his activities and an evidentiary basis that serves as a window into his personality is a lengthy book that he later wrote and whose text survives to this day. Dollier's hand written book was composed in 1672 and only rediscovered in 1844 by a French scholar. It is an indispensable tool. Just as the *Jesuit Relations* were the Jesuit version of events recorded and published in France, Dollier's *Histoire de Montréal 1640-1672* (Reprinted in English as "*A History of Montréal* 1640-1672" 1928 J.M. Dent, Toronto) serves as an equivalent to the "Jesuit Relations" but though the eyes of a Sulpician and the central figure of this work. **1**

In his book Dollier described himself with some coyness as one of the "victims" selected to travel to Canada. It was perhaps mischievous and consistent with the man's self-deprecating ways to describe himself with that term since New France was a place that he came to love and that he would leave only once after his arrival in order to travel back to France, thereafter remaining in Canada for the rest of his life.

On September 7th, 1666, the ship carrying Dollier de Casson arrived at Québec, in the middle of a war. Of this conflict more will be said later. For the moment, let the reader travel forward three years after Dollier's arrival in Canada to the year 1669 when he received the letter from de Queylus informing him of the slave's story. Having travelled the previous year to the Nipissing territory with his fellow Sulpician Michael Barthélemy for the express purpose of learning their language Dollier radically changed his plans and saw this new venture as a "*God given opportunity.*" Dollier devised a plan to travel to the Ohio country up until this point he planned on travelling with his companion and fellow Sulpician, Barthélemy. **2**

Upon receipt of the letter from his Bishop, (it must have taken some time for its delivery as the return route up the Ottawa River was against the current and involved many portages) Dollier seized upon the opportunity. He even developed a friendship with the slave who it now appeared was about to proceed on a state sanctioned trip back to his homeland. It is implicit that Nitarikyk surrendered the day to day control of his slave to Dollier. Dollier left the lands of the Nipissing and headed for Québec. This meant that Dollier, not for the last time would have descended a significant portion of the Ottawa River by canoe and then downstream passing Montréal on the St. Lawrence (this time with the current in his favour) and on to Québec. Events were unfolding rapidly.

Dollier's purpose in leaving the Nipissing territory and travelling to Québec showed a strong commitment to the concept. Funds had to be assigned and supplies purchased. These were not available in sufficient quantity in Montréal. **3** By the year 1669 there was a regular traffic of small sailing vessels going up and downstream the St. Lawrence River between Québec and Montréal. Although canoes might have been used for the passage there were larger vessels that would have permitted Dollier to conveniently bring his supplies back to Montréal from their place of purchase. The use of large flat bottom craft was not possible west of Montréal because of the Lachine rapids. Importantly, permission and written orders were necessary before such a venture into the Upper County, the *Pays d'en Haut* could be undertaken.

These orders came from two sources. Firstly Orders issued from Abbé de Queylus as Dollier's Superior. But of equal significance were the orders to be granted by the Royal Governor of New France Daniel de Remy de Courcelle, a man who had already figured largely in Dollier's earlier experiences in Canada. **4**

When Dollier arrived at Québec three years earlier in 1666 the Colony was in a state of war. The Governor, Courcelle was about to lead several thousand soldiers and men through Iroquois territory in a scorched earth policy meant to blunt or end Iroquois attacks, specifically Mohawk attacks on New France. Coincidentally Dollier took passage to Canada sailing with another Sulpician Priest by the name of Jean Cavelier, the elder brother of René Robert (Cavelier de La Salle) whom we shall soon meet in this work in greater detail and who figures largely in this story.

By 1666 the Iroquois attacks had gone on for years and were principally directed against the French posts at Montréal and Trois Rivières, but in fact no Frenchman was safe anywhere in the countryside. What the French described as "depredations" by the Iroquois had finally reached the ears of King Louis XIV who in 1665 sent a Regiment of regular soldiers to Canada, the Carignan-Salières Regiment, whose task it as to deal with the Iroquois.

These regular soldiers numbering almost one thousand, had in large measure sailed directly from France. In addition to the men of that Regiment were also four companies of soldiers who had first sailed with Courcelle to the Caribbean and attacked Martinique and other Islands to drive out the Dutch and then left that warm climate to join with the other forces at Québec. All these men were trained in European style battle with European style needs and in no way were they ready or equipped for a Canadian Winter. They suffered horribly. The Iroquois for their part avoided pitched battle but lost many of their large villages, which were burned along with supplies stored for the approaching winter as the French marched through upstate New York. Only a few of Courcelle's men had or knew how to use snow shoes (*les Raquettes*) a failure that could not be lost on anyone in attendance, including Dollier.

Temporary forts had been built by the French along the Richelieu River as supply depots. That northward flowing river empties into the St. Lawrence River near Montréal and served as the direct route to the heart of Iroquois and specifically Mohawk territory. It was here that Dollier made his first significant mark. As a Priest Dollier was attached to the military force sent out by Courcelle (the modern term might be "embedded") along with a few other priests who were available and willing to go. Dollier was one of their Chaplains, or *"Aumônier "*as the French called him. No doubt Dollier's former military experience was known by many even though he wore a Priest's vestments.

When the small garrison at a Fort Ste. Anne near the head of Lake Champlain (of all such forts, Ste. Anne was located furthest into Iroquois territory) was about to perish in the deep of winter from illness and want of provisions they sent word of their needs to Montréal. Only one priest came forward to take part in the relief force and in effect, to take leadership of it, and that was Dollier.

Arriving at the garrison, he organised relief and administered what fresh food there was, quickly overcoming the rampant scurvy that had struck the men. He remained at the site and continued to arrange for relief for the men until all were finally returned to Montréal. This was his first lesson in over-wintering in Canada and provided a script of what was needed to survive. It also firmly established his reputation among the soldiers of the Regiment, a reputation that would still be remembered three years later in 1669. All these things would have been known by Governor Courcelle when Dollier attended upon him seeking permission to go on a mission to where no European had travelled, for the purpose of the salvation of souls. Dollier would travel into the unknown and as mentioned he thought at this early stage he would travel with his fellow Sulpician and student of the Algonkian language, Michael Barthélemy.

Dollier presented himself to the Governor at Québec and as his former military Chief Courcelle approved the concept of a voyage to the Ohio country but with one significant condition. Dollier and his party were not to travel alone. They were asked by the Governor himself to accompany another group of men with a very secular purpose. This latter group were to be led by a man whose name would be known to Canadian history as René Robert Cavelier Sieur de La Salle.

Other than what the slave had told them of his homeland what did the French know of the region or the route to get there? The slave had told them only that it would be a voyage of seven hundred to eight hundred leagues.

There is a rich inventory of early maps of Canada from the fanciful and purely imagined ones, created by those who had never seen the lands portrayed, to those possessed of relative accuracy and suggestive detail. The great Champlain was many things and he was a very great navigator and explorer. He relied not only on what he had seen but also incorporated what the Natives told him. His last map drawn in 1632 detailed the northern route to Huronia (specifically the lands between Georgian Bay and Lake Huron, a region of which he and his contemporaries were very familiar) and included a roughly drawn Lake Ontario…or *Lac St. Louis* as he called it. (see further comments in Chapter Eleven)

Based on markings on an earlier map, it is possible that Étienne Brulé descended the Grand River in the early part of the century but Brulé was no chronicler and he left no map. Neither did Fathers Jean Brébeuf (who was burned at the stake by the Iroquois in 1649) or Pierre Joseph Chaumonot who had spent the winter of 1640-1641 in Central Southern Ontario with the Neutrals, prior to the latter's destruction and dispersal by the Iroquois. **5** Brébeuf and Chaumonot left no record of having reached Lake Erie. Dollier may have had some verbal descriptions available to him from Chaumonot. Pierre-Joseph-Marie Chaumonot (1611-1693) was also Aumônier or Chaplain to the Regiments in the 1665 expeditions against the Mohawk. It is reasonably likely that he and Dollier had some contact thereafter and prior to the commencement of Dollier's 1666 duties as Chaplain. Although Chaumonot did not see Lake Erie, he did visit the adjacent lands and appears to have heard Native descriptions of the lake. **6**

Figure 5. Champlain's map of 1632 showing Lake Ontario and depicting Lake Erie as two small lakes.

Equally possible is that the well-educated Dollier had read the only "travel guide" available to the French in that era. Published in 1632 *"Le Grand Voyage au pays des Hurons"* was essentially a best seller for the time, written by the

Récollet Gabriel Sagard. Sagard (also known as Théodat) detailed in a book his journey to Canada and Huronia in 1623-1624. In his detailed text Sagard opined on native food, housing, snowshoes and even wine. Even though there is no direct evidence showing Dollier read it before departing France, it would be surprising if he had not given the notoriety, availability and uniqueness of the text.

There also existed a map. It was called the Sanson map (see Figure 6 below) and Galinée would make express reference to it in his Journal. The Sanson map would have been studied by Galinée prior to his arrival in Canada. In addition to pastoral matters, mathematics, astronomy and cartography, Galinée was a man who knew how to take and record latitude and as well how to note his general longitudinal location by dead reckoning.

Drawn by Nicolas Sanson, (1600-1667) a man who never visited New France, maps such as his were widely published and disseminated in Europe. These maps were pieced together from earlier maps, verbal accounts and raw hearsay. As one author (Heidenreich: *Cartographica*. p.xii) describes it, men like Sanson were "professional map compilers." It was all they had.

Champlain had heard tales about a body of water (Lake Erie) to the south and west of Lake Ontario. As figure 5 shown above depicts, in his last map of 1632 Champlain drew Lake Erie as two small lakes but with no specific details. In Sanson's map, Lake Erie appears in a crude form based on what Natives had verbally related to the French as well perhaps from illegal traders, the Coureurs de Bois. 7

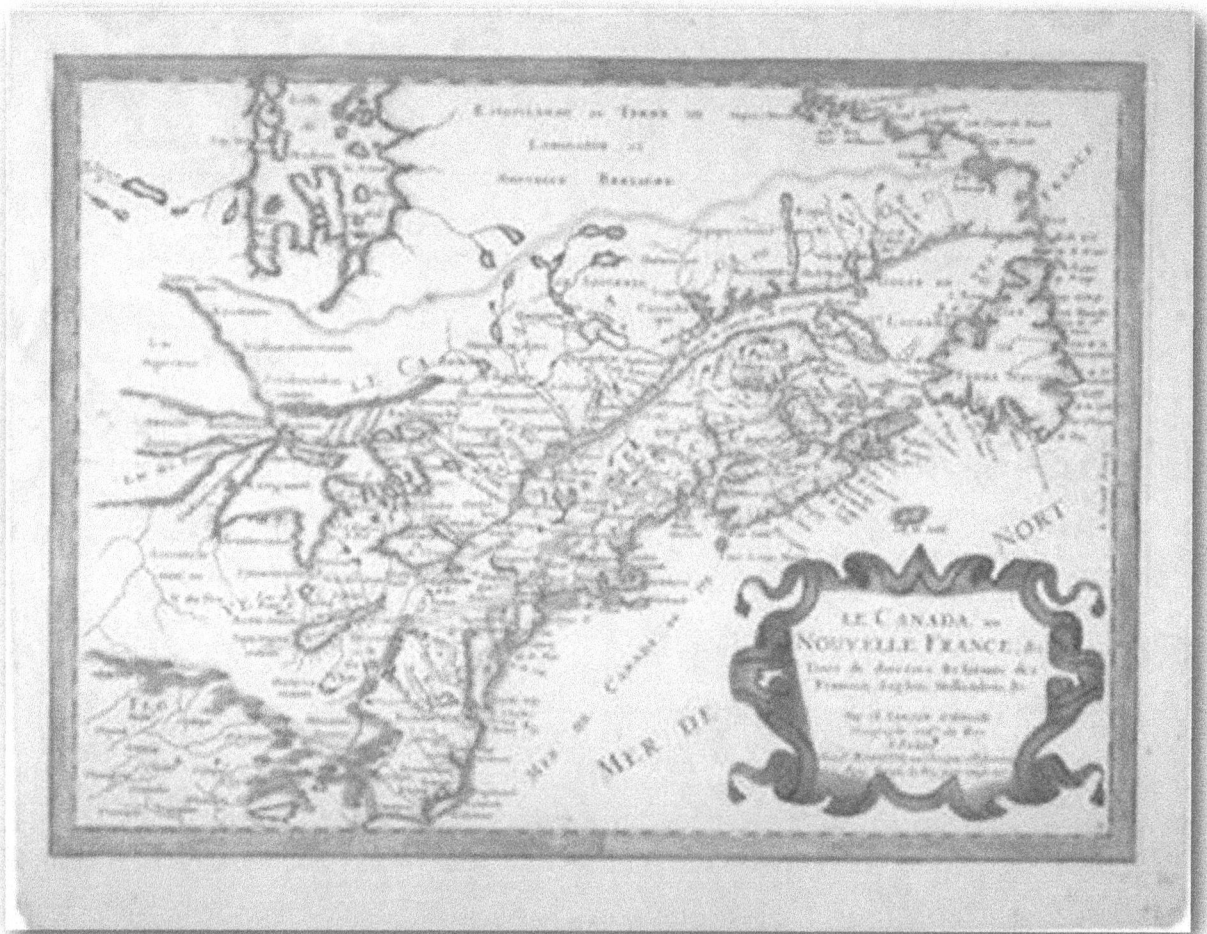

Figure 6 Sanson map of 1650.
Sanson was a French cartographer trained by the Jesuits. The map Galinée knew was but
one of many maps and atlases Sanson would produce during his life.

Native descriptions could be reasonably accurate and were often relied on in great degree until such time as the French passed through the territory themselves and made their own observations. It is possible that rogue fur traders had seen Lake Erie but there was no accurate European "record" of the Lake. Dollier would change the status quo. Like Chaumonot and Brébeuf years earlier, initially Dollier's mission was to be a *voyage-volant*, a "flying trip" to discover the tribes the slave had described and to survey the ground for future proselytizing.

In his quest to befriend the slave who had met de Queylus, Dollier "extracted" from him a promise to guide the Sulpicians back to his own country. It could not have been a difficult promise to extract from him. However, having travelled earlier to the Nipissing country for the express purpose of learning the Algonkian language, Dollier knew he would need an interpreter for the Iroquois language.

Although Iroquoian speaking bands could reasonably understand each other and the same was largely true amongst Algonkian speakers, as between Iroquoian and Algonkian languages, the two were mutually unintelligible. Knowledge of Algonkian was of no relevance in learning and speaking in Iroquois. Dollier thus recruited as one of his party a Dutchman, who would be known through all history via Galinées Journal simply as "the Dutchman" and nothing more.

Galinée later commented that only too late did he *"recognize more than ever how important it was not to engage one's self among (the Natives) without knowing their language or being sure of one's interpreter."*

The Dutchman's (or *Hollondais* as Galinée calls him) name is not revealed in Galinée's Journal but his importance to Galinée is clear in that our Sulpician adventurer realized the necessity of having an Iroquois interpreter. This individual whose provenance was obviously with the former Dutch trading post of Fort Orange, was able to convey that he knew quite perfectly the Iroquois language however the challenge was that he had great difficulty in expressing himself in French.

One is left wondering how Dollier could know of the man's abilities in Iroquois if he spoke little French and the Sulpicians did not speak Dutch. Since there would be a need and an ongoing role for native guides on the journey, interpreting would be important. Language was going to be an issue.

As for La Salle, he continued to assure Courcelle and all who would listen that he too had a good command of Iroquoian. Many accepted this assurance on his part. In what is the only mild criticism of Dollier uttered by Galinée (a criticism that Dollier must have agreed with as he read Galineé's Journal and accepted its contents in preference to his own version) the latter wrote that Dollier's zeal for the mission prevented him from seeing that La Salle was proceeding blindly. The other Sulpicians viewed La Salle with great scepticism. This was the first sign of an embryonic mistrust of La Salle that would manifest itself in the final composition of the Sulpician party.

The Sulpicians, as touched upon earlier in this Chapter, were specifically selected by Courcelle to make the voyage as an offset to the powerful and influential Jesuits. When Champlain first arrived in Québec in 1608 and for a number of years it was the priests of the Récollet Order who were the only "Black Robes" to be found in Canada. Thereafter the very efficient Jesuits exploded on the Canadian scene, even though their numbers in Canada were never very large. They were superbly organised however and very committed in their roles. The Jesuits were seen by the French court as a quasi-political power whose first allegiance was to Rome. Hence to a degree, the employment of the Gallic oriented Sulpicians was a counter-weight to the power of the Society of Jesus. This belief was shared by both the Governor of New France, Courcelle and by the Intendant Jean Talon. In fact in 1666 after his brief and disastrous winter expedition against the Iroquois Courcelle sought to blame the Jesuits in part for his lack of military success by their failure to provide Algonkian guides in a timely fashion.

Authorities in France feared the power of the Jesuit Order that had established itself in Canada and Europe and had reached around the Globe with missions in India and China and Japan. The secular French powers feared their influence as well as their ultramontane allegiance to Rome and non-adherence to the Gallician Church. The Sulpicians were comparatively newer on the scene and carried no such political baggage. Their success could only be in the interest of the secular State, particularly as the mission was funded by them with no expense to the government.

One author (Dechêne at p. 9) notes that "The Jesuits…did not equate conversion (of the Natives) with assimilation…" The Sulpicians were more dogmatic in their dealings with the Natives. Suffice it to say the two orders, Jesuits and Sulpicians had very different approaches to conversions and interaction with the Natives, a difference of approach that was known and exploited by the French government.

Neither the Jesuits not their predecessors earlier in the century, the Récollets, had achieved any significant measure of success in the conversion of Indians. This failure had not as yet been as deeply experienced by the Sulpicians as by others and according to Galinée it was hoped that these Natives of the Ohio would show a greater *"docilité"* than those Natives encountered so far. Part of the Sulpician desire to outreach to distant lands was because they too had not produced any significant results in terms of conversions on the Island of Montréal until that time.

The journey was to be many things, a voyage for profit from La Salle's perspective. It was to be a fulfillment of his vocation for Dollier. But it was also a political trip with the political touch of a distant French Government at play originating from the inner circle of Louis XIV in France. The Court at Saint-Germain-en-Laye wanted something far more valuable that canoes filled with furs. They wanted information. Intendant Talon would later write the King Louis XIV that…

"Since my arrival I have dispatched resolute persons, who promise to push further inland that has ever been done, some to the West and Northwest of Canada, and others to the south and Southwest. These adventurers are in all events to keep journals, and on their return to answer to the written instructions I have given them."

Galinée would fulfill this instruction.

The lands La Salle sought had been described only verbally by the Natives and appeared to correspond with the general destination of Dollier. It was reported by the Indians that the river led to the ocean and they gave it the Iroquois name of the "Ohio". Until he had been requested by Courcelle to accompany La Salle, Dollier had been quite content to go alone accompanied only by those of his choosing.

La Salle's express purpose was to obtain beaver pelts and a route to what was called the Vermillion Sea, a body of water that could lead to China. The Europeans clearly had no idea of the size of the vast continent they were living on. La Salle had been pressing the Governor by a series of speeches and as La Salle was funding his efforts on his own and at no expense to the government Courcelle gave his permission.

For his part, the Intendant Jean Talon was hopeful that exploration of the Interior, the *Pays d'en Haut*, would reveal a shorter and more economical route to transport potential mineral wealth (copper in particular although any gold would have been welcomed) to Montréal instead of the northern Nipissing-Ottawa River route.

The permission to make the journey was such a valuable commodity that it was evidenced by Letters Patent under the signature of the Governor himself and which could be presented to any English authorities La Salle might encounter. Courcelle specifically authorized Dollier to accompany La Salle and to go to the Ohio. Ironically it would be La Salle who would utterly fail in his mission and abandon Dollier while the resolute Dollier would persevere in his non-commercial enterprise and succeed in a way he had not imagined.

It was at this time that Courcelle gave permission for soldiers to leave the ranks and join the expedition. The fact that Galinée specifically noted Courcelle's decision strongly suggests that all seven of the men who ultimately accompanied Dollier were soldiers, that is to say men who had been subject to military discipline and whose habits of discipline would be needed for the journey. The promise of adventure, better pay, profit and escape from the boredom of garrison duty must have produced a considerable line up of applicants. In the end result, seven soldiers became for the moment ex-soldiers and were selected and assigned to Dollier's group. They must have been chosen with considerable care and with an eye to some pre-existing or potential paddling and hunting skills. As events would show, others who were less fortunate joined La Salle's group.

Abbé de Queylus, who also extended permission for the journey was evidently in some degree a close judge of men and their characters for it was he who formed suspicions concerning La Salle, his commitment, skills and depth of character. Divining that La Salle might quit the journey, de Queylus foresaw the need to have someone with mapping and navigational skills. Thus the decision was made by de Queylus that Barthélemy would not be going, rather Galinée would replace him. Publically, the reason recorded by Galinée was that Barthélemy was needed at Montréal for his Algonkian language skills but replacing him with the Sorbonne trained and mathematically skilled Galinée speaks to the Bishops vision that someone would be required to supplant whatever skills La Salle had, or did not have. In his *"History of Montréal"* (see bibliography) written in 1672-1673, Dollier would state that Galinée in fact approached de Queylus and asked if it would not be more *"suitable for him to go."* Further permission for the voyage came not only from de Queylus, Dollier's immediate Superior, but also from the ultimate ecclesiastical authority in Canada, the formidable Bishop Laval. Francois de Laval (1623-1708) was the Jesuit trained Vicar Apostolic for New France at Québec. During the time of our narrative he was the only Bishop in Canada but his actual title was Bishop of Petraea in Arabia! He was Bishop *in Partibus Infidelium*, in the land of the unbelievers.

This fiction and this title did not require Louis XIV's approval and was granted directly by Rome. Later in 1674 Laval was named Bishop for New France when the King and Pope Clement X agreed on the need for such a bishopric and the person to fill it (see End Note 3 for Chapter 11 concerning this and the role Dollier's journey may have played in the establishment of a Bishopric in New France). Laval was not a member of the Society of Jesus but was looked upon by them most favourably. By and large throughout his career he successfully skated through the politics of intrigue that existed between the Jesuit Order and the Court of Louis XIV.

Figure 7. The caption at the top of the image reads " Canadien with snowshoes going to war on the snow." Sketch circa1722 from La Pothierie, *Histoire de l'Amérique Septontrionale.* The seven soldiers with Dollier were likely similarly equipped.

Although in conflict with de Queylus to some degree over matters of jurisdiction Laval stayed above the fray and became a towering influence in New France. His name is memorialised in the many good works he did with a City and a University named after him. Laval was of the view that, as between the Governors, Military Commanders, Intendants and Bishops, the former three would come and go but he and his office would be the thread of continuity and peace between the Jesuits, Sulpicians, Récollets and the lay clergy. He gave the voyage of Dollier his blessing.

Travelling together against the strong current of the St. Lawrence River, La Salle and Dollier left Québec and arrived at Montréal to buy the canoes they needed. Two priests plus seven released soldiers would constitute the Sulpician contribution to the expedition for a total of nine men. La Salle planned on travelling with fourteen men plus himself in five canoes including, according to one source, a surgeon. **8**

It was by now the end of June 1669. The days were long and the summer solstice approached with the inevitable advent of winter in six months time. Yet still they had not departed, nor would they for a few more days. Firstly, three men had to be executed.

Figure 8 René Robert Cavalier Sieur de La Salle.
From a Nineteenth Century French Engraving.

HENRI'S STORY
L'Arrivée

I had joined the Regiment in Orléans. We marched to our ships that were to take us to Canada, a place I had heard of. I had never been to sea and the voyage was terrible. We were very cramped in the ship's hold and men died as we crossed over the ocean. The smell was terrible. Our drinking water quickly turned bad. I mention these things as upon our arrival in Canada I vowed that I would remain there and never chance a return to France. As God willed it, I would break this vow. We were gratefully received by the people of Québec and paraded before the Governor before embarking again to a place called Montréal where the Kings enemies, the Iroquois, committed outrages against the colonists.

We passed the winter at Fort Ste. Anne close to a river called the Richelieu and nearly starved. It was only because of God's will and the intercession of Père Dollier that we survived. The Holy Father arrived at our fort at the time of our deepest despair and by sending for fresh food and with his ministrations we survived. I survived. It was then that I took the measure of this remarkable man and would have followed him anywhere, even to the ends of the earth. When my Regiment returned to France there were a few companies of men who remained in Canada. I was one of them. When I was in garrison and learned that the Holy Father was seeking men to accompany him on a voyage into the wilderness I asked to go. By then I had some experience with the forest and hunting and I thought I had mastered the art of paddling the birch bark canoe. I had much to learn. But being resolved to go I was allowed to leave the garrison and join the Father and the others. I had little idea what would follow.

CHAPTER 3

Galinée and La Salle

———

'Messieurs Dollier and de la Salle went up to Montréal again, after making their purchases at Québec,
and bought all the canoes they could, in order to be able to take as large a party as possible.

JOURNAL OF GALINÉE

A MURDER WOULD BRIEFLY DELAY the commencement of the voyage of Dollier and Galinée to the unknown lands of the south as there were men who had to be executed before the expedition could set off.

Three soldiers of the Montréal garrison had murdered an important member of the Seneca tribe for his furs. The precarious peace with the Iroquois that existed since late 1666 following the conclusion of their latest war with the French, demanded that justice be done and be seen to be done. Crimes by soldiers in the garrison were very common and they were subject to a severe code of discipline.

Murdering a Seneca warrior was perhaps one of the most serious crimes possible as it threatened to destroy the peace and unleash a massive Iroquois response. It was thus that Governor Courcelle ordered the public execution of the three soldiers in front of the Natives so all would know that French subjects and to some degree the Natives were under the protection of French law. The Governor expected that word of this example of French justice would travel though the native community. In the coming months he would be proven correct.

The condemned men asked that Dollier delay his departure so that he could attend to them as their Priest as they awaited their execution. There were many other priests the condemned could have asked for. They wanted Dollier. Their specific request which was granted to them and speaks to the high regard in which Dollier was held by soldiers of the garrison, a reflection no doubt of his earlier interaction with the soldiers during the Iroquois war.

The three day hiatus to address the execution of the three soldiers had another repercussion for it was during this narrow time period that de Quelyus, already suspicious of LaSalle and his capacity to fully engage in the expedition gave effect to those suspicions. Barthélemy would not be going. Thus the twenty-four year old Galinée was given three days notice to prepare.

Galinée was given orders to make a "trustworthy" map as the instructions to Dollier contemplated that after arrival in the Ohio country Galinée would return to Montréal with his map and for provisions to re-supply what would be an new outpost for God in the wilderness.

Galinée was born in 1645 in Rennes in the south west of France. His family were reasonably well off. He was accepted into the Seminary of Saint Sulpice in August 1661 and spent the next seven years there studying and obtained a Degree from the Sorbonne while also studying mathematics and astronomy. Galinée was exceptionally well educated for the time. This was the age when following Galileo's example   (although it resulted in the latter being put under house arrest) astronomers had turned their early telescopes to the night sky to discover that the moon did not have a smooth surface and that Jupiter had visible moons that orbited that planet. These revelations shook Europe and the established Church view of an earth-centric universe.

Galinée arrived in New France as a Deacon (un Diacre) of the Order of Saint Sulpice in 1668. His immediate concern was to learn the Algonkian language and he set about to do so upon his arrival in Montréal.

The scholastic and practical abilities possessed by this young man were obviously identified by his Superior, the Abbé de Queylus. Dollier would have had little opportunity to come to know Galinée prior to the journey to the Ohio Country. Arriving at Québec in 1668 it is only just possible that he met Dollier who was then embarking to the Nipissing Territory from Montréal to learn Algonkian.

That his writing skills as reflected in his Journal were of a force and substance sufficient to be sent to France at the journeys conclusion and being adjudged by Dollier as being superior to his own efforts reveals that Galinée possessed a practical degree of observation that would interest the Royal Court itself. His map and its commentaries held the same characteristics as his Journal and would ultimately be sent on to France as soon as they were prepared.

Galinée was not an experienced paddler. He was not an experienced woodsman. He would become one in short order. As events would demonstrate, de Queylus had chosen Dollier's companion with great wisdom. Galinée would be the counter weight to another member of the expedition, one whose motives and purposes were vastly different than those of the young Sulpician Deacon....La Salle.

La Salle was new on the scene in New France. He was a former Jesuit seminarian who at the last moment had declined to take holy orders in France and instead came to Canada to seek his fortune. La Salle was a complex man who led a complex life. Like all complex men he had his detractors and his supporters, both then and now. He would eventually play a role in the theater of history in a way that was and remains significant both to Canada and the United States. He was driven, ruthless, inquisitive, inspirational and at times duplicitous. For the purpose of our saga, we see La Salle at the earliest stage of his New World career that would later blossom when he obtained the patronage of a future Governor of New France, Louis de Buade de Frontenac. But that lies ahead of the time of our narrative.

La Salle was born in 1643 at Rouen, Normandy into a reasonably wealthy family. At age fifteen he entered the Jesuit College and for almost a decade received there the benefits of an advanced education. The contrast between the young La Salle who took his initial vows in 1660 as a novice Jesuit priest and the adventurer he would become in later years is striking. Like most Jesuits he taught, both at Tours and Blois. Becoming bored, he repeatedly asked to be sent to one of the overseas Jesuit missions, either in China or in Annam (Vietnam) but met with repeated refusals from his Superiors. They saw in him a lack of resolve and other personality issues including a bad temper and a confrontational attitude with authority figures in the Order. However bright he may have been, these latter attributes were not the making of a good Jesuit.

At his request, in the Spring of 1667 he was released from his vows and turned his back on the Jesuits. When his father had died his family's money had gone to a brother (as La Salle could not inherit while he was still bound by the Jesuit vow of poverty) and thus he needed to build his own fortune. No longer requiring permission to travel, in the Autumn of that same year he voyaged to Montréal in New France where his brother Jean was a member of the Sulpician Order.

With his brother's assistance, he obtained a significant grant of land on the west end of the Island of Montréal and became known as Sieur de La Salle taking the latter place-name from property near his ancestral home in France. Essentially, he named himself if not as a member of the local lesser nobility then to a more honourable status than he would ever have been able to achieve in France. In what could be styled a Seventeenth Century land-flip, shortly thereafter he sold most of his land back to the Sulpicians even though he had paid nothing for it.

La Salle planned to use these funds to discover the Ohio, la Belle Rivière and perhaps another greater river as yet unknown to Europeans (the Mississippi) and he was desirous to go on a voyage of discovery. He must have been a convincing speaker to gain the ear of Courcelle and he must have possessed significant bravado as he asserted that he could speak Iroquois sufficiently well to converse with them even though he had been in New France for only two years. His duplicity on this matter would land at the doorstep of Dollier and cost La Salle a great deal of money without any profit in return.

Once provisions had been carefully selected and stowed in their fragile craft it remained only for the men to carefully mount their canoes and begin a very lengthy voyage that few modern men or women could physically accomplish.

So the journey began with great optimism on the part of the Sulpicians, and great expectations and need for profit on the part of La Salle. It began also with a common belief held by those left behind in Montréal that none of the travellers would ever be seen alive again.

Henri's Story
Préparations

We prepared as best we could. Father Dollier and the Abbé de Queylus provided us with all we would need and could carry in our three canoes. We had to be careful to take only what was necessary. Apart from the clothes on our backs we took one set of heavy clothes for the winter. We had spent enough time in Canada to know that the warmth of summer would be followed with the hellish cold of winter.

We were able to take with us the newer flintlocks, the musketoons we had been issued with as soldiers in France. They were a godsend as many of the soldiers in the garrison had been obliged to send them back to France after the peace with the Iroquois and were armed only with the old weapons, the wheel locks. We could never have hunted with the necessary stealth required should we have had the older firearms as they were slow to fire and the game could escape. The canoes were full of powder, shot, flints, and weapons.

The fathers had their Holy Chapel, and many gifts for the Natives. Our axes, spare paddles and other necessities meant that each man was wedged tightly in our canoes. The canoes were of the best quality but even so it was always in my mind that it was only the thickness of the bark that separated me from the dark waters we paddled through and that like all of the other men, I could not swim. So I put my faith in God and gave the prospect of drowning little thought, which became easier to do each day after we had embarked.

CHAPTER 4

Departure & Ascent of the St. Lawrence

————

Saturday, July 6th 1669
Ville Marie Island of Montréal
45 ° North Latitude
73.5 ° West Longitude

THE DAY OF DEPARTURE ARRIVED. It was July 6th, 1669. The bodies of the three executed soldiers still swung from the posts at the shoreline where they had been shot by a firing squad. Dollier remarked in his *History of Montreal* that the condemned men *"paid for their crimes and put themselves in the hands of God with admirable resignation."* The canoes of the living were fully provisioned with little freeboard to show. Each canoe carried as much as they could, consistent with safety, while carrying the necessities of survival, such as gunpowder, shot, axes and only a little food as sustenance would have to be the product of an ongoing hunt. In protective wrapping was the Altar and Chapel set. The chalice and other articles for performing the Mass were central to the daily life of the Priests and to the core purpose of their mission. They had one such set to celebrate the Eucharist …but only one set.

Dollier's three canoes set out. Five other canoes with La Salle and his men and two canoes of Senecas acting as temporary guides also left that summer day. As part of the group was the slave previously held by Nitarikyk, the very slave whose story had begun this saga and the unnamed Dutch interpreter. Whether they would find the Vermilion Sea, the Ohio River, or engage in the salvation of souls was unknown to them. But they believed in their cause. No such expedition had ever continued on westward beyond the confluence of the Ottawa River and the St. Lawrence River.

They would be the first Europeans to travel so far into the Iroquois lands in such numbers. They would not be the last.

Galinée wrote…

"Our fleet, consisting of seven canoes, each with three men, left Montréal on the 6th of July, 1669, under the guidance of two canoes of Seneca Iroquois, who had come to Montréal as early as the autumn of the year 1668 to do their hunting and trading.

With the outfit I have mentioned, we left Montréal on the 6th of July, 1669, and the same day ascended the St. Louis Rapids, which are only a league and a half away. Navigation above Montréal is quite different from that below. The latter is made in ships, barks, launches, and boats, because the River St. Lawrence is very deep, as far up as Montréal, a distance of 200 leagues; but immediately above Montréal one is confronted with a rapid or waterfall amidst numerous large rocks, that will not allow a boat to go through, so that canoes only can be used."

Unbeknown to them they would paddle their canoes thousands of kilometers. Equally unknown at the outset was the fact that of the Sulpician party of two priests and seven soldiers, all would survive a voyage lasting almost one year. That they did would be due in large measure to the leadership, knowledge and resolve of Dollier.

Traditionally, the French would have travelled a short distance west of Montréal and turned right or roughly north-bound up the Ottawa River. This time they continued west on the St. Lawrence, or as it was also known *"La Rivière des Iroquois"*…the River of the Iroquois. Crossing Lac St. Francis and Lac St. Louis, Galinée, who among the entire group would have been a novice paddler, described the route as extremely difficult for almost two hundred Leagues. They found themselves hugging the shoreline and often times in the water dragging the canoes.

Even at this early stage, while ascending the St. Lawrence River illness struck the group, but there was no weakening of resolve to push forward. Fish were plentiful and their diet was supplemented by two moose they shot. **1** The moose were good to eat but the heat of the summer quickly spoiled what they could not cook. Pausing to smoke the meat for preservation was not part of the plan. The summer days were long and hot and the distances to be travelled stretching out almost limitlessly. Although smoking their meat was done later in the journey, at this stage they could not pause to clean the animal, chop the wood, and smoke the meat. There was no time. Always present on their minds was the passage of time and the approach of winter in lands that would be completely unknown to them. They had to keep moving.

Paddling occupied their entire day. With three men in each canoe pushing against the St. Lawrence current their rest came only at days end when…

"…you find towards evening the fair earth all ready to receive your tired body. When the weather is fine, after unloading your canoe, you make a fire and go to bed without otherwise housing yourself."

Should it rain at night the space for the men to sleep under the shelter of an overturned canoe would be limited. One can feel the aches in their arms and shoulders as each morning broke and the endless rhythm of paddling in unison began once again.

They were in Galinée's words, even at this early stage of the journey, *"miserable."*

On Friday, August 2nd, they came to the source of the St. Lawrence River…Lake Ontario. This fresh water lake came into their sight appearing as though a great sea. Stories told to the French by the Natives describing other greater seas to the west must have been substantially corroborated by the appearance of this great lake, otherwise unknown to most Europeans.

Figure 9. Painting by Frances Hopkins "Voyageurs at Dawn" 1871. Although of a later era and showing larger canoes than our traveller's, the painting depicts the scene for sleeping at night as Galinée described.

Completing their ascent of the St. Lawrence, Dollier had contemplated travelling to Kenté near present day Kingston where the Sulpicians had recently established a small Mission. **2** Dollier expressed his wish to follow the north shore of Lake Ontario to its western end but the Seneca guides would have none of it and they were firmly in control at this moment.

Arriving at Lake Ontario the two canoes piloted by the independent minded Seneca made it clear that they intended to travel along the south shore to their home villages and had no intention of taking a detour along the north shore. As Galinée wrote…

"We dared not leave our guides (sic) lest we should be unable to find any others."

Only months before a small party of Jesuits had travelled to the Iroquois lands south of the Lake and were soon reinforced in their mission on the Onondaga River (in the vicinity of modern Syracuse New York). Galinée knew that the south shore of Lake Ontario was the home territory of the Five Nations. Until recently, it had been "enemy" territory. The lands of the Seneca's Mohawk brothers which lay to the east had been ravaged by Courcelle and perhaps by some of the very soldiers in the canoes of Dollier and Galinée. For the moment there was a state of uneasy peace.

It was noted by Galinée that they felt in danger for their lives the entire time they were in the vicinity of the Five Nations. That danger would not lessen as they probed deeper into the lands of the most warlike and most populous of the Tribes, the Seneca, or as the French called them the Tsonnontouans. Galinée and the others were well aware that the peace had only been made very shortly before and that individual acts of violence by young warriors could not be prevented solely by a treaty made by old men (*par les viellards*).

News of the murder of the Seneca warrior at Montréal and the execution of the three French soldiers had reached the area. Although Galinée believed that the bulk of the Seneca nation was appeased by the execution of the perpetrators he was mindful that some of the deceased's family may not have felt that the crime had been fully expiated. Dollier therefore had the men *"perform sentry duty every night"* and they kept their weapons in good working order.

It was the nature of the Iroquois Confederacy that no clan actually gave up its right to take independent action and no person did either. A consensus arrived at between a Clan and the French, or between the Clans was just that, a consensus. According to Galinée and Iroquois practice *"everyone is perfectly free in their actions"* so that someone who lost a relation in the preceding war or a relation of the murdered Seneca might feel free to act against the French.

There was awareness of danger but no fear on the part of the Missionaries. Galinée wrote that in the midst of all of the fears he knew they were there *"par la volonté de Dieu"* by the will of God. He declared the purpose of their presence was to save the souls of these poor *"savages,"* while at other times referring to them as *"barbarians."* If the French occasionally perceived the Natives as barbarous the sentiment was mutually held by the Natives towards the Europeans who scarcely had the wherewithal to survive in the forest and who regularly performed a ceremony that concluded, from the Native's vantage point with the priests eating part of their god while denying the Natives the right to occasionally eat their conquered enemies.

The Sulpician's faith was complete and unshakeable. Their commitment to their Church and its doctrine was total. Twenty-First Century questioning of the Seventeenth Century Church or religious beliefs and foundations is unhelpful for the modern reader. The mission of Dollier and Galinée can only be understood if appreciated through the lens of history. These men were absolute in their beliefs and their resolve. In their worldview they and their Church alone held the path to eternal salvation. The Natives lived in ignorance and had to be informed, reformed and saved. Modern respect for differing cultural beliefs and values was a concept that was irrelevant to Dollier and Galinée and if expressed outwardly in Europe could still result in one being burned at the stake.

On August 8th the party arrived at a small encampment on an island inhabited during the summer month by a single Seneca male and his family. Two days later their guides left them for the main Seneca village and to notify the inhabitants of the impending arrival of the French.

Dollier was sick with a fever and near death.

It might be recalled at this point that whatever distance the group had travelled since their departure from Montréal, within that calendar Dollier had travelled much farther. His "travel-year" had begun in Nipissing territory with the descent of the Ottawa River to Montréal, followed by a journey to Québec and thence back to Montréal to begin the voyage. Perhaps it had been even too much for any man however strong. Pressing on towards the Seneca village, Dollier anticipated that his own death was near but felt that his work in the wilderness rendered him as close to his Sulpician brethren as though he were at the Seminary of Saint Sulpice in France.

For the moment they moved on in a westerly direction without guides but following the south shore of the lake. Anyone with any experience in a canoe can imagine the difficulty encountered and the skill employed in paddling parallel to the shore with heavily laden canoes and waves striking the sides of the canoes at a right angle. The days were still long. Paddling began at first light and did not end until shortly before dark. Their sense of time must have been very different from ours today. It was not a time of instant communication or next day accomplishment. Their worldview was profoundly different than ours.

On August 26th they arrived at Karontagouat near modern Rochester New York and the Genesee River. The great Seneca village of Ganondagan was inland from there.

Galinée paused and with considerable precision took his position of latitude using his Jacobs Staff. His measurement using this device was largely accurate down to minutes and seconds of arc. His cartographic skills of observing and recording were already in use.

Figure 10. Man using a Jacob's staff to measure latitude. Galinée was well versed in the use of this device to determine his latitude as its basic principles had been known in Europe for over 300 years.

Natives from the village arrived at the lakeshore with a variety of fruits and vegetables that would have been familiar to a modern person and a life saver to the weary Frenchmen. The French gave as gifts to the Natives presents of knives, awls, needles and other things they would value. Of these gifts they were well provisioned. Clearly their earlier preparations in Montréal had included sufficient gifts and goods for exchange for the Natives. All these things were valuable but were competing all the same for space for weapons, gunpowder and shot and other essentials in their frail canoes.

It was at this moment the Seneca began a strategy that would cause a significant delay. Advising the Frenchmen that they would only speak through a Council of Elders the Natives bade the French to wait a day while the Elders from three other nearby villages assembled at Ganondagan and that the Elders would then approve or disapprove of the reason for the Frenchmen's arrival.

There was at this stage some strategic collaboration between La Salle and Dollier. It was decided that Galinée would go with La Salle to the village located inland while Dollier remained at the lakeshore protecting the canoes with all but ten men, while he recovered from his illness. Galinée and La Salle also had it in their minds to acquire a slave who could act as a guide. Galinée even opined that the slave would ideally originate from the one of the tribes they wished to visit.

They could not know as they travelled away from the shore of Lake Ontario southward to the interior and the great Seneca village of Ganondagan that they would witness there a ritual torture and an act of cannibalism.

Henri's Story
Mon Travail

Nothing I had experienced in New France had prepared me for what I went through. As strong a man as I believed myself to be from marching and cutting wood, paddling the canoes every day made my arms feel as though they would separate from my body. My back hurt and yet I said nothing for fear of ridicule from my comrades. At no time did the Holy Fathers relent or slow down or complain and they paddled just as hard as any of us, all former soldiers. They even let us sing our songs even though some of them would make an honest man blush. We ate only a little but did not stop. We paddled against the current of the river of Canada. We paddled in the heat. We paddled even while swarms of insects attacked us. But we did not stop by day. At night we ate and slept the sleep of the dead only to be roused by the sounds of the Fathers at their morning prayers. Then at first light we started paddling again.

I began to doubt my decision to join the Fathers but strangely, after several days it all became part of my life and the days took on a rhythm I can still feel today even after all these years. Two of the men suffered pain and swelling in their groin but Père Galinée made them a truss of cloth which they wore and they were much improved by this.

At last we came upon a great inland sea, yet the water was fresh and abundant with fish. I was told it was Lac St Louis. I asked if it was our destination but the others only laughed and shook their heads. The Holy Fathers just smiled.

CHAPTER 5
Canoes and Paddlers

"I have made a long digression here upon canoes because, as I have already said, I have found
nothing here more beautiful or more convenient. Without them it would be impossible to
navigate above Montréal or in any of the numerous rivers of this country."

GALINÉE'S JOURNAL

ONLY RARELY IN HISTORICAL NARRATIVES can facts be asserted with complete certainty but this fact is certain. Canoes were an invention of the First Nations. No European could have travelled to the interior of North America without total reliance on these remarkable vessels.

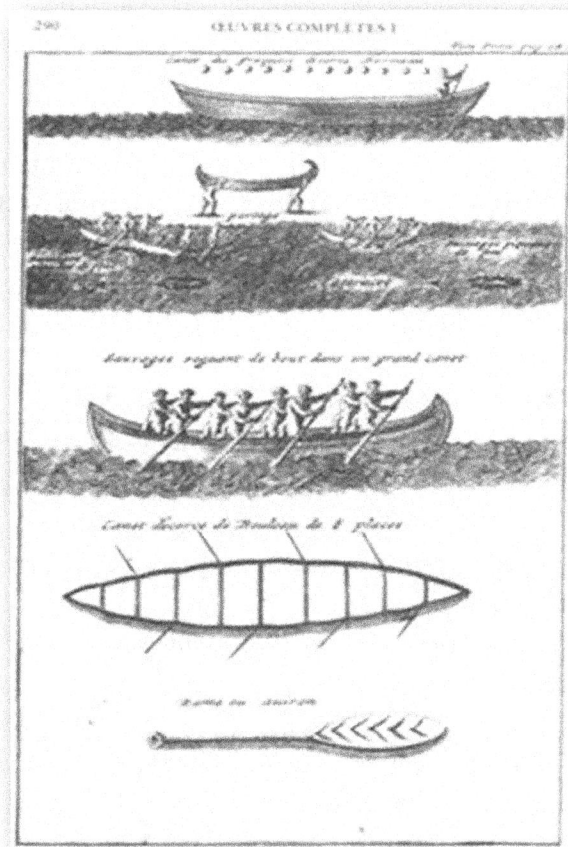

Figure 11. Native Canoes from Lahontan. See Endnote 1 for this Chapter.

To have an understanding what it was like for our travellers, one must have some appreciation of the remarkable vessels that were the principal form of transport…the canoe.

An analogy between canoes and modern manned-spaceships has some merit. Both spaceships and canoes are complex technical examples of the engineering capacities of their time and perform their function well most of the time. Canoes and spaceships are and were both relatively expensive to purchase. Both are strong yet fragile. Given the limited cubic footage in each canoe, necessarily allowing for the men, the provisions and a measure of freeboard between floating and drowning, it might be said that no Apollo spacecraft of the Twentieth Century was packed with any less care than these watercraft plunging into unknown waters. The final truism is that if seriously damaged, the consequences to the traveller in either a spacecraft or birch bark canoe would likely be fatal.

Many readers will have paddled a canoe in calm waters and run it on to the shoreline. Canoes of aluminum, composite and cedar are now the order of the day. It was very different for Dollier and company. Writing in the 1680's, Lahontan cautioned concerning the handling of birch bark canoes that…

"…if they (the canoes) *do but touch or grate upon stone or sand the cracks of the bark fly open, upon which the water gets in…"* (Lahontan volume 1, p 27) **1**

Maintenance of the canoes was therefore critical but also time consuming and required access to forest gums and saps which were themselves only seasonally available and dependant on the composition of the local forest.

For every item added to a canoe (or a spacecraft) it meant something else could not be taken because of the finite cubic space in the vessel. Careful planning for a voyage into the unknown required thoughtful deliberation with redundancy built in. No spacecraft today would have but one computer system because if it failed the mission would be a disaster. No canoe expedition would carry only one firearm for hunting as it would likely have the same effect, when the loss of a firearm meant there would be no hunt and thus no food.

Galinée wrote complaining that the purchase of his canoe cost him the staggering sum of eighty Livres (roughly the equivalent of a senior army officers pay for a month) having purchased it from a Frenchman. Had he been able to purchase it from the Natives he believed it would have cost him a lesser sum of 10 crowns equivalent in goods and not in specie. Lahontan noted the price of a new birch bar canoe in the 1680's was 80 Crowns but that even then they would only have a life span of five or six years (Lahontan volume 1, p. 29).

Galinée spent considerable time in the Journal describing the canoes, their use, repair and their protection from the elements.

This is part of what Galinée had to say in describing their canoes…

" These are little birch-bark canoes, about twenty feet long and two feet wide, strengthened inside with cedar floors and gunwales, very thin, so that one man carries it with ease, although the boat is capable of carrying four men and eight or nine hundred pounds' weight of baggage. There are some made that carry as many as ten or twelve men with their outfit, but it requires two or three men to carry them.

This style of canoes affords the most convenient and the commonest mode of navigation in this country.… These canoes cost Frenchmen who buy them from Indians nine or ten crowns in clothes, but from Frenchmen to Frenchmen they are much dearer. Mine cost me eighty livres. It is only the Algonkin-speaking tribes that build these canoes well. The Iroquois use all kinds of bark except birch for their canoes. They build canoes that are badly made and very heavy, which last at most only a month, whilst those of the Algonkins, if taken care of, last five or six years.

You do not row in these canoes as in a boat. In the latter the oar is attached to a rowlock on the boat's side; but here you hold one hand near the blade of the oar and the other at the end of the handle, and use it to push the water behind you, without the oar touching the canoe in any way. Moreover, it is necessary in these canoes to remain all the time on your knees or seated, taking care to preserve your balance well; for the vessels are so light that a weight of twenty pounds on one side more than the other is enough to overturn them, and so quickly that one scarcely has time to guard against it. They are so frail that to bear a little upon a stone or to touch it a little clumsily is sufficient to cause a hole, which can, however, be mended with resin.

The convenience of these canoes is great in these streams, full of cataracts or waterfalls, and rapids through which it is impossible to take any boat. When you reach them you load canoe and baggage upon your shoulders and go overland until the navigation is good; and then you put your canoe back into the water, and embark again. If God grants me the grace of returning to France, I shall endeavor to take over one of these canoes, to show it to those who have not seen them. I see no handiwork of the Indians that appears to me to merit the attention of Europeans, except their canoes and their rackets for walking on snow. There is no conveyance either better or swifter than that of the canoe; for four good canoe-men will not be afraid to bet that they can pass in their canoe eight or ten rowers in the fastest launch that can be seen.

I have made a long digression here upon canoes because, as I have already said, I have found nothing here more beautiful or more convenient. Without them it would be impossible to navigate above Montréal or in any of the numerous rivers of this country."

Much of the expeditions paddling would be done along the shores of Lakes Ontario and Erie, with the vessels crammed with provisions and items essential to their survival yet with just sufficient freeboard to keep the canoes from being swamped by waves. With three men in each canoe the freeboard must have been negligible in canoes that were but twenty feet long and two feet wide (Galinée actually uses the word *"pieds"* or feet as a unit of measurement).

Each of the three men in the canoe would have a specific paddling function. The man in the bow, the *"avant"* would be expected to keep a close eye for rocks or submerged logs that could put a hole in the vessel. The center man, the *"milieu"* was simply expected to add power. The rearmost man, the *"gouverneur"* had the task of paddling like the rest but also to steer. In time specialized paddle sizes and shapes would be developed for each function but this specialization is only known to have existed among later fur traders in the 18th Century.

Lahontan described the paddles of the era in the following way…

"The oars they make use of are made of Maplewood…the blade of the oar is 20 inches long, six inches broad and four lines thick. The handle is about three feet long."

In each canoe three paddlers would make their strokes in unison. It is also likely that the entire group would often paddle in unison, governed by the rhythm of song because if each canoe was paddled at its own rate eventually all the canoes would stretch out over unmanageable distances. Safety and security were paramount for camping overnight. In short, they needed to stick together.

Dollier had even equipped the canoes with small sails which were occasionally used (strung from the paddles) when there was a following breeze and very calm waters. Tacking was impossible so that the use of sails, although mentioned, was very infrequent. Hernias were common among all Voyageurs and Coureurs de Bois and a truss was the usual remedy. According to Lahontan (Volume 1, p. 28) the men would paddle on their knees and sometimes, when calm waters permitted, from the higher vantage point of a sitting position.

The rate of stroke was likely similar to modern usage and absent wind or waves would be approximately fifty strokes per minute. The reader can contemplate at their leisure how they might feel paddling at that rate over a twelve to fourteen hour day under a summer sun while under attack by insects.

The strain of paddling would have been intense particularly when paddling against a current such as on the St. Lawrence and other rivers they later encountered. The current of the St. Lawrence is always strong but following the laws of physics, grows stronger whenever the river narrowed suggesting that at those places the travellers must have hugged the shore as often as they could as there is no suggestion that they ever portaged during their ascent of that river or later the Detroit River or the even longer St. Clair River.

Nighttime meant the canoe was carefully landed, unloaded and in some cases upturned to provide shelter from the rain and partial shelter from the clouds of mosquitos (as per Figure 9). This practice, mentioned earlier was noted by Galinée even at the early stages of the journey when they were ascending the St. Lawrence.

Lahontan, travelling a part of the same route several years later noted…

" Every day there is some chink or seam (of the canoe) to be gummed over…at night they are always unloaded and carried on shore where they are made fast with pegs, lest the wind should blow them away." (Lahontan, Volume 1 p. 27)

Europe had nothing like the birch bark canoe. The common feature of roads in Europe was that they were appalling and difficult to travel most of the year. In Europe the age of canals had barely begun. North America had highways…. and many of them. They were not the concrete pathways that so occupy our modern lives, rather they were the lakes and rivers and their tributaries stretching into the interior of the continent. The various lakes and rivers can be fully analogized to modern concrete highways. They were however seasonal, freezing up as the particular season and latitude might dictate.

The river passages were possessed of great strategic and logistical significance. It was easier by far to move one thousand pounds of goods ten miles by water than one mile by land. The land was almost completely forested. There were some large meadows to be sure or as the French called them *"prairies"* creating occasional breaks in the canopy of the old growth forest that covered parts of Ontario's temperate regions. But the forest remained largely impenetrable and very difficult to transit when it came to carrying large packs or bales of furs. There were some First Nation pathways through the forests but these land pathways did not permit other than short distances to be covered or relatively light loads to be carried.

Rivers and lakes were the expressways of the day, but speed and distance travelled varied daily dependant on current, wind, waves, water level and the number of paddlers, their skill, strength and fatigue. But it was easier and faster than walking through the maze of forest.

Portages were not to be looked forward to. A portage meant one had to safely land the canoe and unload it either completely (a portage) or partly so as to permit the canoe to be dragged (a décharge). The traveller would have to carry the canoe a distance (Galinée noted that one man alone could carry an emptied Algonquin built birch bark canoes) and then move the contents separately only to reload the canoe again. Each of Dollier's three canoes carried up to nine hundred pounds of supplies.

Portaging took time. It was necessary to portage to avoid rapids or shallow waters but it inherently delayed arrival at ones' destination. Portaging also carried risks. Our traveller's longest portage would occur in the Autumn of 1669 but was executed with considerable assistance from the Natives. Thereafter in 1670 the portages they encountered entailed a staggering effort due to the nature and number of them required to access Lake Nipissing and to descend the Ottawa River.

There were two great water highways that led to the interior of North America. The first to be discovered was the St. Lawrence River leading ultimately to the Great Lakes. In 1534, when Jacques Cartier stood at what would be the future site of Montréal, he could not know as he looked down river that the water flowed from rivers flowing from the far west of Canada, to Lake Superior and thence down the St. Lawrence.

The existence of the Great Lakes and the fact that they were connected was only hinted at almost a century after Cartier and then only by First Nations who gave verbal descriptions of Lake Ontario and a fresh water sea beyond. Initially the French did know that this fresh water sea was accessible by the Nipissing route.

The only other water highway which permitted entry to the interior of the undiscovered continent was Hudson Bay, named after the erstwhile Dutch explorer. In 1611 Henry Hudson had the misfortune to have his crew mutiny and set him, his small son and a few others adrift in that body of water in a small ship's boat, to die of cold and hunger. Hudson's geographic legacy rests with the Bay named after him which would in time become a battleground between the French and English empires.

Lands were held in common within the tribal bands, and occasionally overlapped with other tribes. Trading monopolies were not held in common. Remaining as the middlemen of trade was essential to the Iroquois. It was after all their homeland by right or conquest and above a tribe or band was a kinship group that included those who were born into it, married into it or were adopted into it. The sight of the French travelling down their water-highway must have disturbed the Iroquois greatly.

As we return to our narrative, one can consider the innermost thoughts of Galinée, the refined and well educated Frenchman whose world was so very much defined by the canoe in which he paddled for he wrote in his Journal that… *"When a person is in one of these (canoes) he is always not a finger's breadth, but the thickness of five or six sheets of paper, from death."*

There courage and resolve was manifested in their trust and reliance on their canoes. In the text and Dollier's later History of Montréal there is strong evidence to infer that none of the men could swim.

The immediate danger they faced at this time came not on the water but on land, at the great Seneca village of Ganondagan.

CHAPTER 6
Iroquois and Northern New York

———

Tuesday August 13th, 1669

The Great Seneca Village

42.96 ° North Latitude

77.41° West Longitude

39 days from Ville Marie

Approximately 500 kilometers from Island of Montréal

"I ran and found (the prisoner) who was to be burned…tied to a stake. I saw an Iroquois apply
his red hot gun barrel to the top of his feet which made the poor wretch utter a cry."

JOURNAL OF GALINÉE

LA SALLE AND GALINÉE ALONG with eight of the Frenchmen set off on August 12th leaving the remainder of both parties on the shore of Lake Ontario with Dollier. His illness would keep him there. He thought he might die. Galinée's group were accompanied by forty or fifty Natives who would stop every five kilometers, so as not to "fatigue" the French. This somewhat patronizing act by the Natives portended what was to come. More and more Natives kept meeting the group and slowing them down with provisions but at last they arrived at the large village.

Describing it as occupying a clearing well over a kilometer wide, the French entered the Seneca village of Ganondagan. **1** This was the largest of the Seneca villages and it was the home of the embryonic Jesuit Mission of St. Jacques. Galinée described it as being built on a hill and being comprised of over one hundred Longhouses surrounded by a palisade of poles twelve to thirteen feet high, fastened together and planted in the ground. The village was perfectly square which in the opinion of Galinée, rendered it indefensible.

Preliminary greetings took place with the Elders and only then were the Frenchmen were allowed to enter within the enclosed stockade of the Village with the assurance from the French that they would disclose the purpose of their voyage. The French were led, surrounded by children and the women of the village, to the largest Longhouse where they would stay. The welcome ceremony was meant to impress the French.

It was not the first time Frenchmen had arrived at Ganondagan. The venerable Jesuit Father Pierre-Joseph Chaumonot had been there in the late 1650's for the purpose of effecting conversions, which he claimed he achieved (Jesuit Relations Vol. 44 chapter XVII 1658) but he did not remain there long and perhaps due to his own illness he never returned.

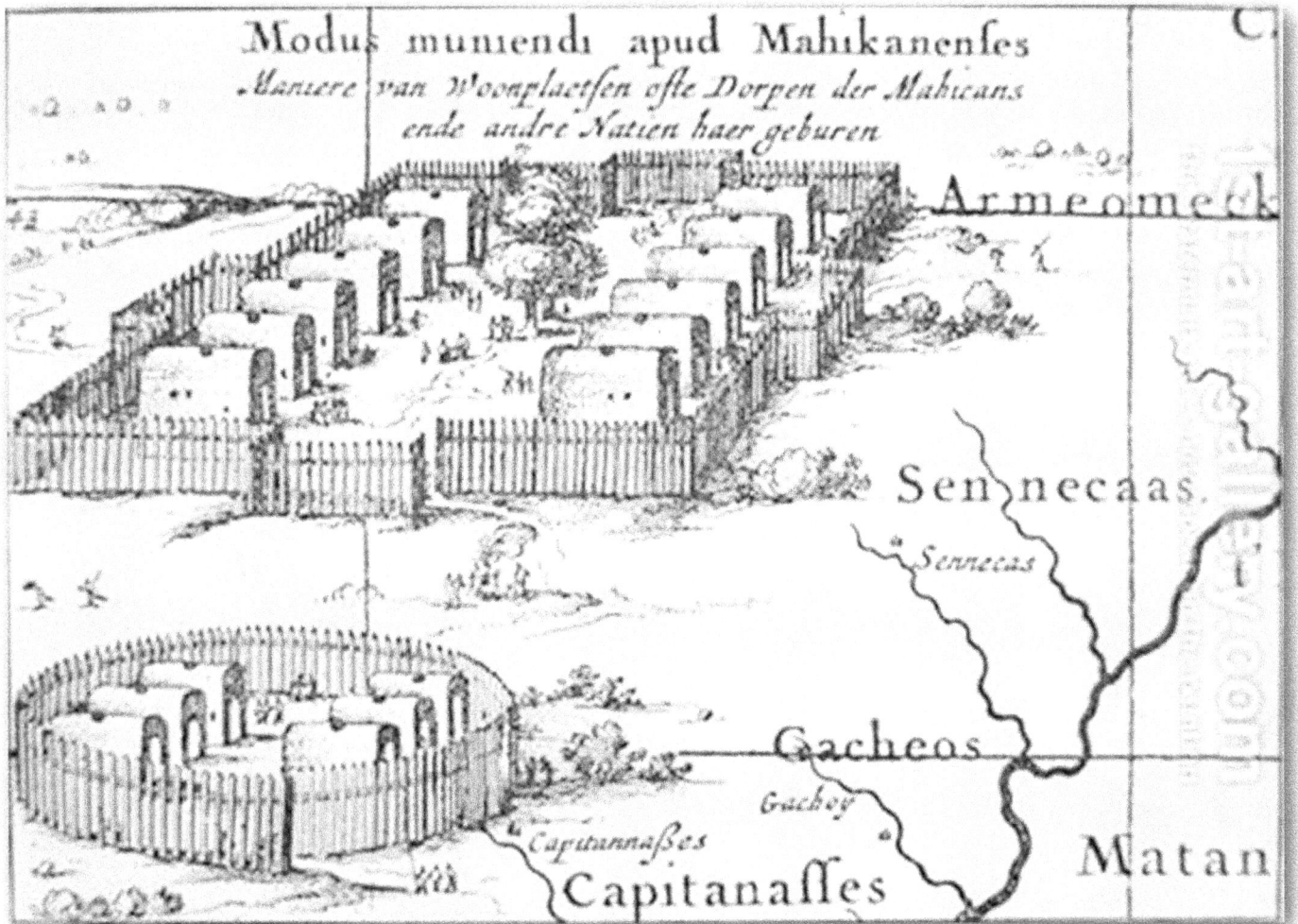

Figure 12. A Dutch schematic of a Mahican Seventeenth Century village. The Iroquois palisades would have been similar. Iroquois Longhouses were much bigger than those shown. The amount of wood required for construction was staggering.

Smoke would rise from the many fires of the Longhouses as multiple families lived communally in these structures. All the inhabitants watched as the arrival of the French was an important event to everyone.

By the evening of the 12th of August not only were local Elders present but elders (*les viellards*) had arrived from three other villages. Clearly the Native "telegraph" had worked quickly and had cast a very wide net. The presence of the Frenchman in their territory was important to the Seneca. For his part Galinée, a man of the Church, did not hesitate to take note of the military capacity of the Seneca in assessing the disposition of the village and the Seneca capacity to raise something in the order of 1200 warriors. These were curious military observations for a man on a mission whose stated purpose was designed for the salvation of souls. The Seneca were powerful and they knew it and so did the French.

On the morning of August 13th no fewer than sixty Elders of the Nation sat in the Longhouse where the French had spent the night. The Elders lit their pipes and kept them lit throughout. It was then that La Salle was obliged to admit his lie. He could not speak Iroquois, not a word of it. He had no means to make himself understood. One wonders what he had expected to happen since he would have known that his unmasking would be inevitable.

The unnamed Dutchman/Interpreter then announced that his French was not good enough to make himself fully understood. However, a timely dose of good luck arrived in the presence of a Native who was the interpreter for Father Jacques Frémin (1628-1691) the Jesuit priest, who would normally be at his nearby mission. Frémin had gone for a few days to Onondaga, (near modern Syracuse) approximately one hundred kilometers distant for a meeting of the few Jesuits who were scattered to the east among the Five Nations. Frémin and the Jesuits had held a tenuous presence in Five Nations territory since 1667 but even less so in Seneca lands. Father Frémin's "man" would interpret. The French remained at the village for almost a month. This was an extraordinary amount of time to pause with the ever mounting pressure of approaching winter and being so far from home. Frémin never would arrive on the scene while Galinée and La Salle were there.

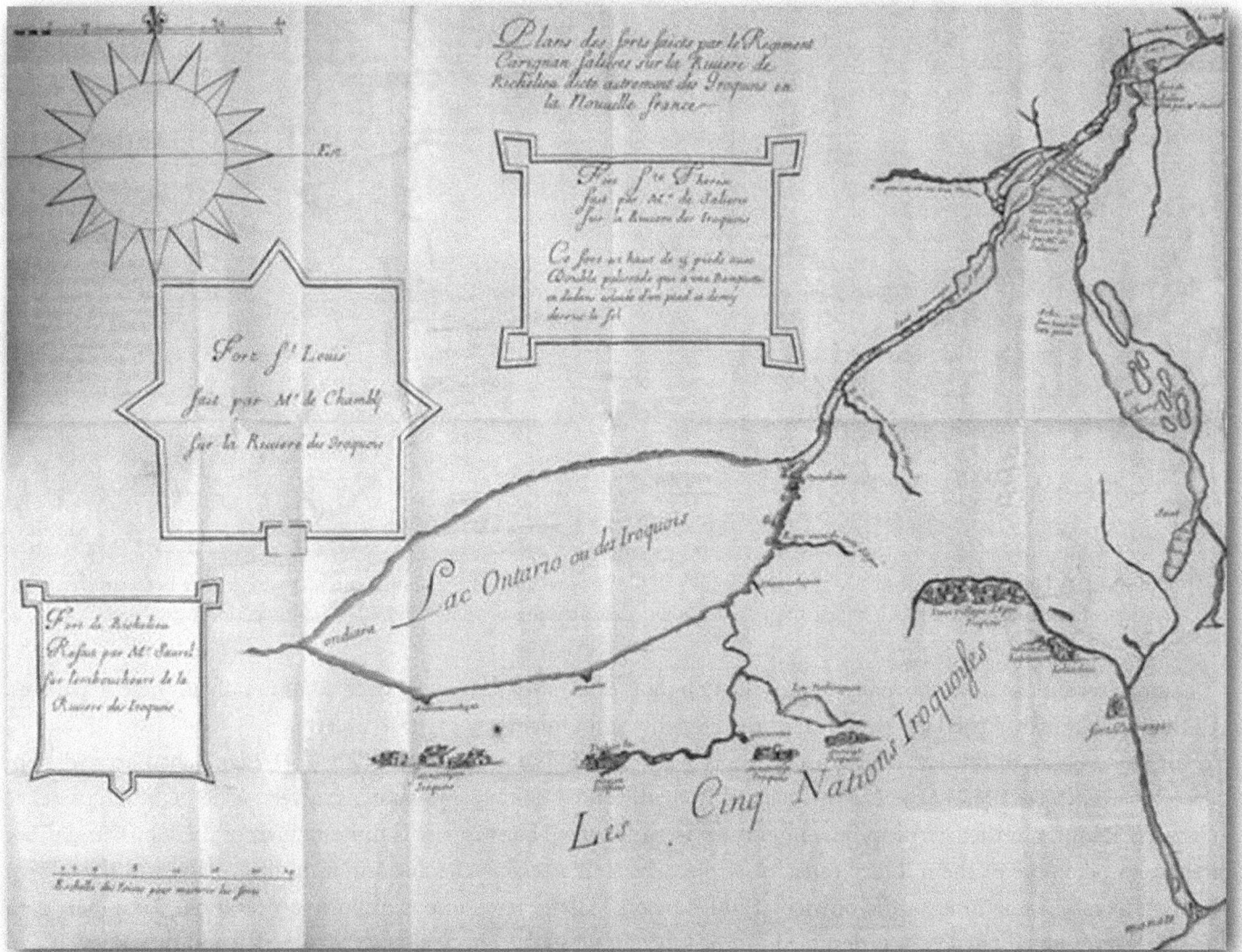

Figure 13. Plan of the Forts built by the Carignan Salieres Regiment showing Ganondagan, inland on the south west end of Lake Ontario. From the Jesuit Relation of François Mercier, *Relation de ce qui s'est passé en la Nouvelle France, lés années 1664 & 1665*.

The three possibilities for Frémin's non-appearance may be stated as follows: firstly, that he was busy elsewhere with his fellow Jesuits, or secondly that the Natives deliberately did not tell Frémin of Galinée's presence so as to preclude a meeting between the two French parties. Finally, one has to consider that Frémin learned of the presence of La Salle's group and chose not to come.

After all, La Salle was an apostate Jesuit. Having joined the Jesuit Order in France he had left the Order and embarked for New France to fulfill his commercial and exploration dreams. The thought of assisting this man, who clearly was not a man of God, and one who was in the company of Sulpicians (that La Salle's brother in Montréal was also a Sulpician would have been known to Frémin) may have meant that meeting his fellow countrymen was not Frémin's first priority.

If this latter hypothesis is correct it would have been but a mirror of the competitive dynamics at play between the Gallician oriented Sulpicians and the Rome based Jesuits whose power (derived no doubt by their efficiencies and hard work) was the subject of envy and suspicion both in New France and in the Royal Court in France. However the second possibility cited above would have been in the Seneca's best interests.

The meeting with the Elders began with a gift to the Natives of a double barreled pistol worth, according to Galinée, some sixty Livres. Such a gift was a curious first step since it showed off French technology in firearms even though the French never had and never would (officially) provide non Christianized Natives with firearms.

Galinée advised the Elders that with this pistol they could with one shot kill other tribesmen with whom they were at war. Evidently included with the gift would be shot and powder. More gifts followed: ten kettles (likely made of copper versus iron due to their weight) twelve hatchets, two cloaks and five or six pounds of glass beads, all given to confirm the recent Peace. All of these goods had consumed precious space and weight in the fragile canoes but were no doubt sourced not solely from the Sulpicians but at La Salle's expense and from his canoes as well. Gifts were the grease to turn the wheel and encourage Seneca approval of French passage through Seneca lands and as well to obtain a slave to guide them to the Ohio. In this the French would fail.

Galinée wrote that it had been La Salle's earlier stated intention to use these gifts to acquire slave from the Seneca to act as a guide. The Elders said nothing in response except that they would consider the request of the French and answer the next day.

On August 14th The Elders gathered again and gave to the French two gifts with the promise of a third. Firstly they presented to the French a wampum belt **2** assuring the French that they considered them as brothers. They certainly did not see themselves as subject to nor inferior in any way to the French. They then presented a second wampum belt to confirm the Peace signed by Courcelle and the Seneca in 1666. Their third "gift" was a bit more vague.

The Elders promised to provide the French with a slave to act as a guide but indicated that because all of their slaves so qualified were off trading with the Dutch at Fort Orange they would complete the gift as soon as one returned. Galinée and La Salle accepted this but urged the Natives to expedite the matter as the season was getting late. To this request the Elders agreed to keep them waiting no more than a week.

Over that following week the Natives feted the French. Feasting was the prime activity even though Galinée complained that one of the principal dishes served was dog. **3** Seven or eight days passed in this fashion.

During this time Galinée and La Salle undertook the role of tourists to fill their time. Galinée wrote that they were taken by the Natives of Ganondagan to visit to a spring that burned when fire was applied to it. Noting that there was a bad odour, although non sulphurous, it must be assumed there was a source of methane feeding into the spring. Galinée called it a Bitumen Spring (*fontaine de bitume*). Its likely location was approximately fifteen kilometers south of Ganondagan or twelve kilometers south east of modern day Canandaigua, New York. The presence of the gas would foretell of industrial fracking three and a half centuries later.

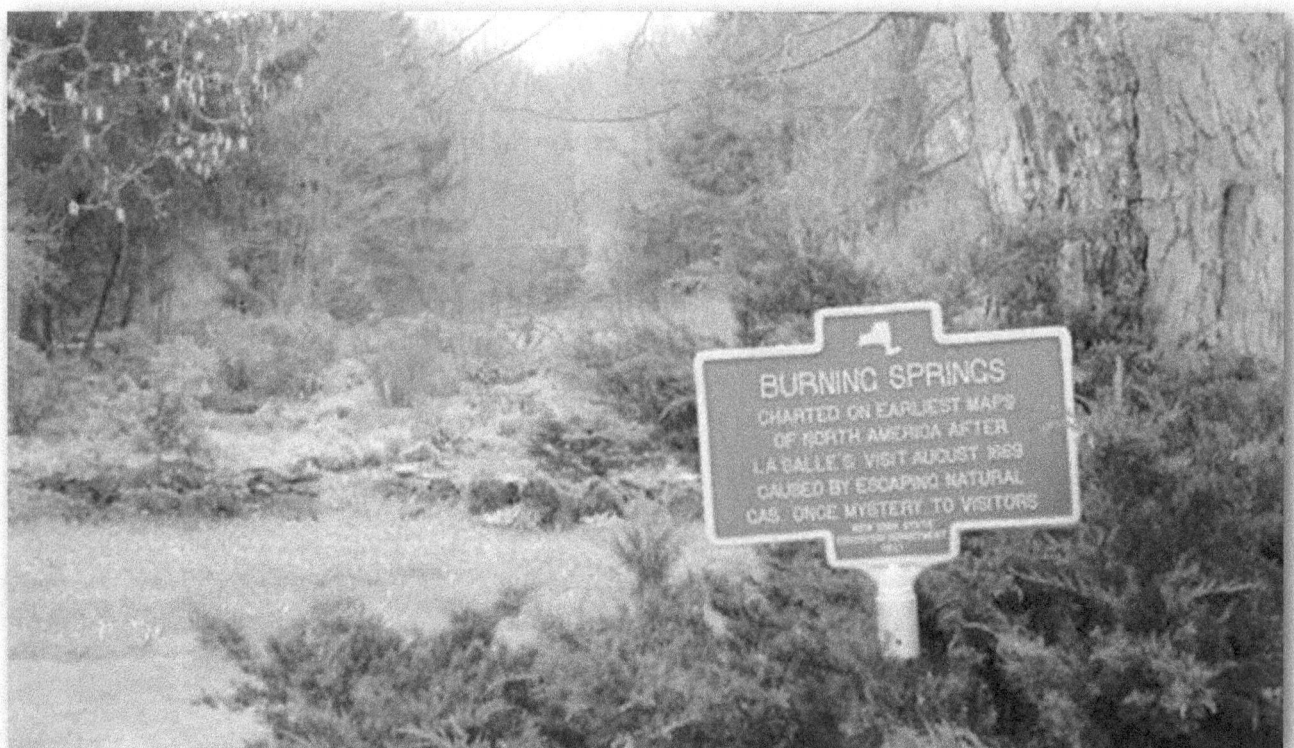

Figure 14. Site of the Burning Spring visited by Galinée and La Salle near Bristol N.Y. It is located approximately 15 kilometers or about four leagues (as described by Galinée) south of Ganondagan. The marker was placed by the State of New York in 1937.

Upon returning to the village they learned that one of the Native groups that had gone to trade with the Dutch had returned with a quantity of brandy. The latter was a commodity that was more potent than wine and more easily transportable in casks, unlike wine which would go bad in casks. The returning party included alcohol, but not the slave/guide as promised. Some of the relatives of the Seneca who had been murdered in Montréal, and whose murderers had been executed just prior to Dollier's departure from there, were themselves inhabitants at Ganondagan and in a drunken state fueled by the Dutch brandy spoke of taking further revenge on those French who were present. Clearly the native telegraph had worked once again as between Montréal in early July and the native village in upstate New York. Equally curious is that to this point the "telegraph" had not worked as well so as to inform Father Frémin of the presence of his countrymen or to the trading parties at Fort Orange directing them to return with a guide for the French.

The Seneca were playing a game of delay. The lateness of the season might convince the French to abandon their mission. The Seneca would have absolutely no commercial benefit from the French probing deeper to the west into their lands. As earlier noted, trading rights were jealously guarded as once displaced as a source of goods or as a middle man the ability of the Band to make any kind of profit or advantageous trade all but vanished. Economic survival was at stake.

The drunkenness fueled by the Dutch brandy subsided and sobriety returned. But Galinée and La Salle kept on guard so that nothing adverse should happen to them either by accident or design. It was at this time that Galinée recorded an event that would unnerve the Dutchman and possibly La Salle even further. Some Seneca warriors had been involved in a skirmish in which one of their members was killed but during which they in turn had captured a member of the Touguenhas, known today as Shawnee. At the time the Touguenhas were in a state of conflict with the Seneca who would raid their lands in the Ohio country and in modern day Pennsylvania.

The prisoner was but eighteen or twenty years of age and he faced certain death preceded by prolonged ritual torture and the prospect of being cannibalized. As a captive, the prisoner had been given to an old woman of the village whose son had been killed, no doubt by the Touguenhas. To expiate her son's death she required the prisoner to die. Galinée sought to obtain the man as the slave who had been promised but Frémin's interpreter, notwithstanding Galinée's threats, refused to put the question to the Seneca and fled from him. The prisoner asked to see the French. 4

Galinée wrote about this event at very great length. A reader of the text might say unnecessarily so. Its inclusion in over several pages of the Journal may have been a form of propaganda designed to paint the Seneca as barbarous and not worthy of the ministrations of the Jesuits or other Black Robes. The details that were recorded could not have come as a shock given the routine judicial violence imposed on convicted criminals in France. On no other topic save only when he wrote extolling the virtues of the canoe would Galinée spend so much time agonizing with his reader, knowing all the while that his readers would be his Bishop, and the Intendant Talon and Minister Colbert in France. He wrote with emotion.

> "*The irons were in the fire to torture the poor wretch. An Iroquois applied his red hot gun barrel to the top of his feet…They* (Galinée's men) *reported next day that he had been burned with hot irons over his whole body for the space of six hours, until there was not a single spot on him that was not roasted. After that they had required him to run six courses through the square where the Iroquois awaited him armed with large flaming brands, with which they kept urging him on and knocking him down when he came near them. Many took kettles full of coals and hot cinders, with which they covered him the instant that, by reason of his exhaustion and weakness, he wished to rest for a single moment. At last, after two hours of this…they killed him with a stone and …tore him to pieces. One carried off his head, another an arm, a third some other limb…to put it in the kettle to feast on. Several presented portions of his flesh to the French, telling them there was no better eating in the world, but no one would try the experiment.*"

That night the Iroquois beat the sides of their Longhouses to frighten away the dead man's spirit lest it had hidden itself in their homes. The modern reader should recall at this point that the Salem witch trials of New England lay in the future and that the Inquisition's tortures in Europe were in full operation. The Iroquois had nothing to teach the Europeans concerning the treatment of war captives. 5

Galinée had given thought to his soul saving task but felt he could not baptize the victim as he had not had time to instruct him given the language barrier. He noted as well that the Iroquois were "pressing" him to leave the prisoner alone so they could begin with their tortures. After the death of the captive, Galinée and La Salle provisioned themselves with Indian corn supplied by the women of the village and travelled approximately thirty kilometers back to Dollier's shore side encampment where there was a smaller Seneca village. At this time they had contemplated taking an overland route to the Ohio but the Seneca at this small village told them that the Lake Erie route would be faster and better.

It was then that first mention of a route via a river to Lake Erie was made. The Seneca also asserted that if they went overland the French risked death from their enemies (the Touguenhas and others) and that if harm came to the French the Governor at Québec might blame them. Thus it became apparent from their hosts that no guide would be forthcoming. The waning ardour of the Dutchman must have been sensed by the Seneca who plied the Dutchman with tales of terror that lay ahead of him, including nighttime attacks by their enemies and near certain death. Having seen what became of the young captive in the Seneca village, the Dutchman would have a graphic image of what could also befall him if captured by hostile Natives.

Plainly the Natives wanted the Frenchmen to penetrate no further behind the "Iroquois curtain." The Seneca put off the French request for a guide from day to day inventing excuses that their departed tribesmen were much slower in returning than expected. Galinée knew. He knew that the delay was too long and that the season was slipping past with the very real prospect that they would not be able to winter with any tribe, but rather would be obliged to winter alone. La Salle expressed to Galinée that such a scenario would be certain death (*une morte asseurée*) for the French. La Salle had no experience in over wintering alone in the wilderness. Dollier did.

Not for the last time, good luck arrived again and just in time for the French. The good luck came in the form of an Iroquois not of the Seneca but of the Lake Ontario Iroquois. This lone native was travelling from Albany having engaged in trade with the Dutch residents there and was returning to his home village of Ganastogué, likely located according to one modern source near the mouth of the Credit River that flows into Lake Ontario. **6** Since the destruction and dispersal of the Huron and Neutral by the Iroquois in 1649, to a limited extent certain Iroquois had established themselves on the North Shore of Lake Ontario. Drawing as well from the Cayuga and Oneida who established themselves near Kenté, some smaller numbers of Seneca settled near modern Toronto and as we shall see, to the east of modern Cambridge, Ontario.

This north shore Iroquois offered to take the French to lands where game was plentiful and where, according to this one man, there were Native slaves from the Ohio lands in a village. Galinée posited that given that the village they were going to was but a small one with eighteen or twenty longhouses the French could impress the Seneca there, through fear, (*par crainte*) to do what the other Seneca would not do through friendship. This Deacon of Old France was prepared to flex muscle in the Upper Country of New France. With the guide providence had given them and the need to ever keep moving, the French set out, or as Galinée put it, they "quit" the Senecas.

It was just in time, autumn was approaching.

Figure 15. Site of Ganondagan, Victor, New York. The reader must consider Galinee's written description. " *At last we saw ourselves in sight of the great village, which is in the midst of a large clearing about two leagues in circumference.... in order to reach it, it is necessary to ascend a small hill. This village (has) a lot of cabins, surrounded by palisades of poles 12 or 13 feet high... for the most part beautiful broad meadows, on which the grass is as tall as myself. In spots where there are woods, these are oak plains, so open that one could easily run through them on horseback".*

HENRI'S STORY
Village des Iroquois

At last we stopped our paddling on the great inland sea but were much delayed by the Indians. We went with our weapons to their village which was like a fort but one made of wood and with many wooden houses inside. Their food did not agree with me for I could not bring myself at first to eat dog but my comrades convinced me to close my eyes and fill my belly.

We saw the Indians most cruelly torture another Indian from an unknown tribe. The women seemed to take the most delight in his agonies until death claimed him. I have seen things almost as bad in France done to those who were Huguenots or fell away from the Church. The Indians I am told never torture their own people as we do, only their enemies.

I thanked God for Père Dollier's recovery from sickness and when at last after too much time had passed the Holy Fathers announced that we were ready to carry on I was glad to leave the place as the Indians seemed suspicious of us and our intentions. Even though it was good to go our path ahead was still unknown and the days were getting shorter. The nights were very cool and getting colder. I sensed that the coming winter was watching us like an invisible spectre, waiting to devour us.

CHAPTER 7
Head of the Lake and Jolliet

———

Friday, September 20th,1669
Burlington Bay, Western end of Lake Ontario
43.23° North Latitude
79.85° West Longitude
77 Days from Ville Marie
Approximately 660 kilometers from Island of Montréal

THE WESTERN END OF LAKE Ontario, known by some as the "Head of the Lake" or Burlington Bay or Hamilton Harbour has to be visualized in 1669 compared with the scene that presents itself today. The roar of traffic thundering over the Burlington Skyway Bridge and the Queen Elizabeth Highway is heard over the sound of Lake Freighters blowing their ship's horns as they enter the channel bringing iron ore to Hamilton's Steel plants. The modern reclamation efforts to save the polluted waters of Lake Ontario's western extremity and the body of water known as Cootes Paradise must be viewed against what was the pristine landscape that presented itself as Dollier and La Salle's party brought their canoes to a stop at or near today's "La Salle Park" in Burlington, Ontario. Galinée described a fine large sandy bay, at the bottom of which was another little lake, namely Burlington Bay.

Years later, in 1795, Elizabeth Simcoe, wife of the Ontario's first (English) Lieutenant Governor, John Graves Simcoe would describe the clear waters of Lake Ontario, as abounding with salmon and lands that were rich in deer, bear and wolves. Today it abounds with high-rise condominiums and cars and trucks.

Having left the Seneca village, the travellers travelled westward and by the mouth of the Niagara River whose current Galinée remarked upon. The Natives had given him a reasonably accurate description of the height of the Falls and their distance from the river's mouth but Dollier's desire to move on to the village kept them from being the first Europeans to actually see Niagara. That would fall to the Récollet Priest Louis Hennepin, (1626-1705) a friend and sometime follower of La Salle's who would be the first European known to see Niagara Falls in 1678. Dollier and his men did however hear the roar of the Falls from the mouth of the river.

Galinée would note in his Journal, that he was later informed by a fellow Sulpician, Father Claude Trouvé (see Endnote 5 for Chapter 8) that one could hear the sound of the waters of Niagara even from the Burlington Bay side of the lake. Given that the Falls then were somewhat further downstream from their current position (erosion has significantly moved the Falls location to the south) and that the amount of water falling then was vastly greater than what a tourist would see today (due to hydro-electric diversion of most of the waters) it remains possible that on a calm day in 1669 one could hear the Falls even from Burlington. Today's tourist visiting Niagara sees but a shadow of what the landscape was like at that time.

Five days from the mouth of the Niagara, after paddling parallel to the shore line, the party came ashore. With respect to those Iroquois they would now encounter, a more robust approach was to be used and was documented by Galinée who wrote…

" *We persuaded ourselves we should all the more easily becomes its masters and make them do through fear a part of what they would not be willing to do for friendship.*"

The approach articulated by an early Twentieth Century American President of "walk softly but carry a big stick" seemed to reflect the diplomatic style the French would adopt.

Moreover, this approach was to be conveyed not only to the Natives but also to the Sulpician's religious and secular superiors. This can be deduced from the fact that Galinée was not writing his Journal for general public consumption. His work was not in the genre of the Jesuit Relations which were published annually and widely read in France, rather it was a report containing impressions and details of interest for the Intendant Jean Talon and even for Colbert in France.

These impressions and comments of Galinée must have been approved of or in accord with Dollier's viewpoint as upon their ultimate return to Montréal, Dollier would write his own account of the journey but upon reading Galinée's, as earlier noted he felt it superior to his own and sadly for history, destroyed his own written account of the trip.

Upon arrival at the Head of the Lake the French faced a not insignificant portage to the village called Tinaoutoua, still eighteen miles (five or six leagues) away. Unloading their canoes at the suggestion of their guide they awaited the arrival of the village Elders. There they waited for three days. It was during this time that that La Salle fell ill or at least reported for the first time that he was ill.

When the principal persons of the village arrived at the lakeshore, along with most of its inhabitants, there was again an exchange of gifts including two slaves that were given to the French. One slave went to La Salle's party and the other to Dollier. It was a curious feature that at this juncture the skills of the Dutchman improved and he found he was able to do much better at translating Iroquois than he had been able to at the great Seneca village of Ganondagan.

To some degree the Dollier-La Salle party of Frenchmen must have taken on a war like appearance. Galinée noted that the Natives were not of a number to resist them and that they begged the French not to burn their village as the French had done to the Mohawks. This was a clear reference to the expedition of 1666 whose scorched earth policy had left Mohawk villages burned and their fields ruined. This mention of Courcelle's attacks on the Mohawks in 1666 shows that the news of the region travelled, endured and was recalled. These North Shore Iroquois clearly did not live in isolation from other events in New France.

A further exchange of gifts followed including a significant amount of wampum from the Natives and at last, accompanied by no fewer than fifty men and women of the village, they set out September 22nd for Tinaoutoua.

Their portage would be their longest portage of the entire journey, and was made possible only by the assistance of the Natives as they ploughed overland through dense bush towards the village that was but five Leagues away. Here was the experiential event proving that transport by water was easier than by land as Galinée recounted how as they moved through the forest their packs would get caught in the trees making them recoil three or four paces. As always, careful handling of their canoes was paramount.

Whatever the causes were of La Salle's illness, his fever must have been objectively observable, or not as the case may have been, to the medically astute Dollier. La Salle returned from a hunt with a high fever that laid him low for several days. He had also experienced a frightful encounter with three large poisonous rattlesnakes (*Serpents à sonnette*) that may have been part of the onset of his illness. **1**

It may have been that the "muscular" approach adopted by the French brought on a degree of enhanced assistance from the Natives of this village. In short, the sooner the French left the happier the villagers would be. To that end they told Galinée that not only would they help the French with their baggage in this lengthy portage but thereafter would show them in short order a river that would swiftly take them south to Lake Erie.

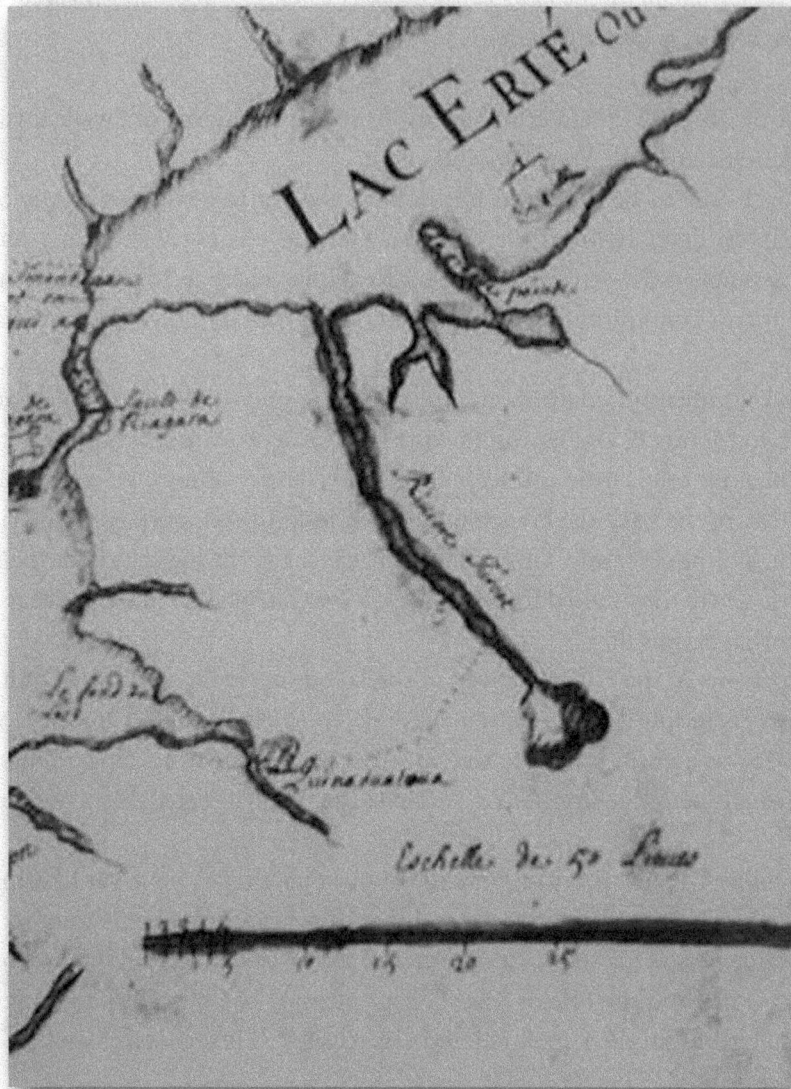

Figure 16. Part of the map of 1688 by Pierre Raffeix drawn eighteen years after our story depicting Tinaoutoua (sometimes spelled Quinaouataoua) at the east end of the dotted line. South is at the top. Note the portage to the Grand and the inclusion of a sailing vessel west of Long Pont, perhaps a reference to La Salle's later construction and loss of the *Griffon*. The future Fort Niagara is also shown.

Dollier in particular was pleased with the inhabitants of Tinaoutoua and with the prospect of reaching the Ohio which, according to the natives, could be accomplished in a month and a half. **2** Dollier then came to a decision even before arriving in the village. In no circumstance would he be returning to Montréal.

As if experiencing his own epiphany Dollier "resolved never to return" and to consecrate the rest of his days to remain among the Natives if he could find any nation willing to receive him. So the plan was hatched that Dollier would remain in whatever new found country they might come upon while Galinée returned to Montréal for provisions and thence return again. How the seven accompanying ex-soldiers felt about this is not known. The first voyage had not been completed yet a second was being planned! Then on September 23rd, while still on portage and the night before their arrival at Tinaoutoua astonishing news was brought to them. There were two Frenchman in the village!

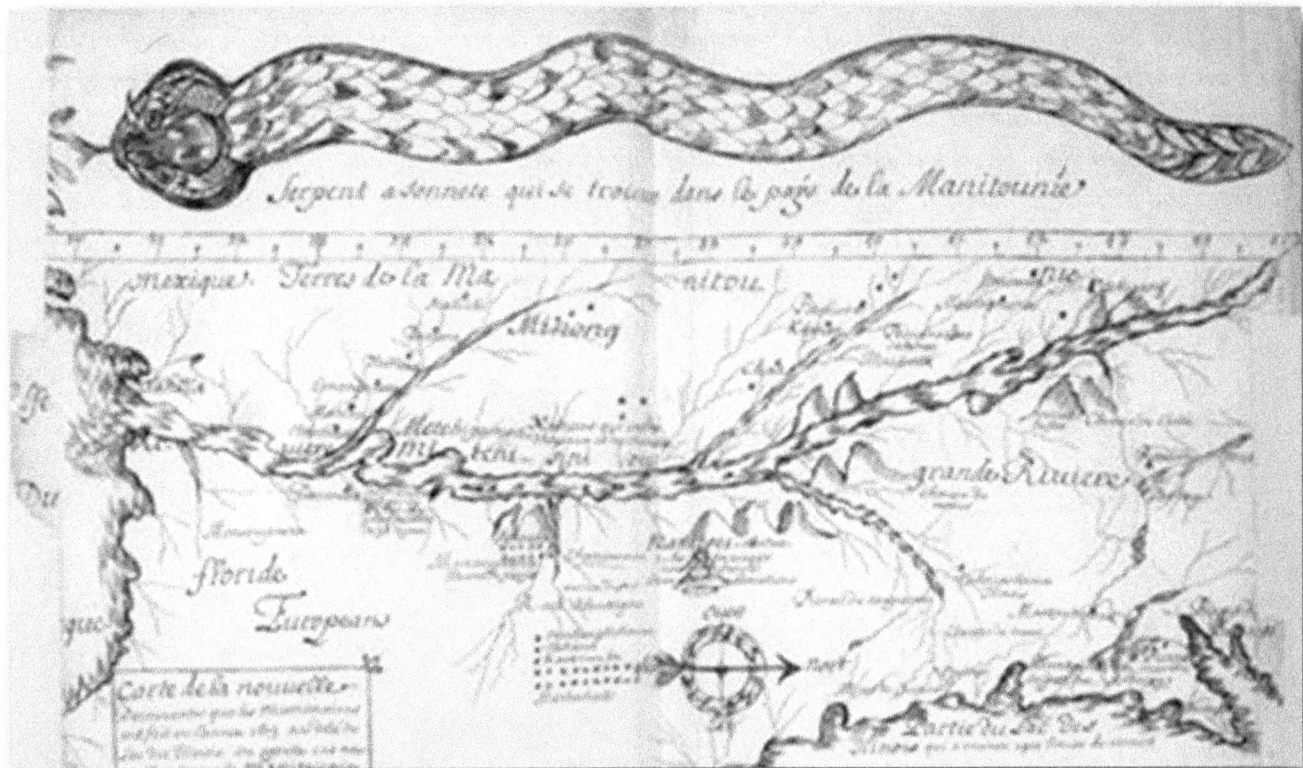

Figure 17 Rattlesnake (serpent à sonnettes) from *Codex Canadensis*
drawn circa 1700 by the Jesuit Louis Nicolas.

HENRI'S STORY
Pays d'en Haut

When we left the large Indian village we continued on to the western end of the great inland fresh water sea. There was a river whose mouth we passed and it possessed a very strong current. The Indian with us said there was a great waterfall up the river and when we camped that night we could hear the sound of the roaring of the water, although we did not delay our passage to see it. I thought it strange there should be such a mighty waterfall when there were no mountains visible from which such a volume of water could fall. At the end of the lake near a large sandy beach we encountered some more Indians who seemed worried that we might attack them and as most of us including M. La Salle's party were soldiers it might have seemed so.

We travelled inland with a number of the Natives who carried our provisions although we carried our weapons and our canoes lest they be damaged through their carelessness for nothing else we possessed short of our weapons and the Holy Fathers Chapel were of more importance to us. At last we came upon a native village but not one nearly as large as the last village we had been at nor did it have a wall around it. The Iroquois there were much fewer in number. Two of our countrymen arrived with a native and we were as surprised as if we had seen a vision…to meet a Frenchman in the wilderness seemed to us as if God had our care in his hands. Père Galinée learned many useful things from one named Jolliet and it was here we celebrated the Eucharist.

It was late in the year and I could tell by the birds and the sky that summer was nearly over. There was nothing I could do but carry on. Again with the help of the Natives we did a great portage of several days. We could not have done this great portage from the fresh water sea without them. This time we took a direct path arriving at another river that flowed south. Some of the Indians seemed anxious for us to depart.

We had learned that M. La Salle and his men would be leaving us at the village and we would travel on alone and without a guide to the land the Fathers had decided to visit. The only Indian guide we had was sent on by Père Dollier with the Hollandais to look for a canoe.

We had been alone before but our party was now reduced by more than half and it took all our faith and the Father's zeal for their mission to carry on. We were completely alone. We were so very far from Montréal and so much further from France I wondered if I should ever see either place again in this life.

CHAPTER 8

Tinaoutoua and Descent of the Grand River

Saturday, September 24ᵗʰ, 1669

Tinaoutoua

43.28° North Latitude

80.00° West Longitude

81 days since departure from Montréal

Approximately 687 kilometers from Island of Montréal

THE FRENCHMAN IN THE VILLAGE was Adrien Jolliet and he had arrived at Tinaoutoua from the west. Born in New France circa 1642 he was the older brother of the more famous Louis Jolliet, who later in his life would discover the Mississippi River for the French. Jolliet had been sent out from Montréal late in 1668 as second in charge of a voyage led by one Jean Peré. Their task, given to them by the Intendant Jean Talon was to travel to the north shore of Lake Superior to determine the truth concerning stories of copper mines there and to see if there was a practical route to bring mineral wealth to New France other than via the difficult Ottawa-Nipissing route. Talon and his political master in France, Minister Jean Baptiste Colbert felt that France was entitled to a share of the wealth of the New World along with Spain, Portugal and England. In particular Talon sought a diversification of the economy of New France to include more than furs and animal skins.

Leaving Montréal in 1668 with four canoes stuffed with goods to trade with the tribe of the Ottawa's near Lake Superior, and accompanied by Jean Père, Jolliet had travelled the traditional route to Lake Superior following the Ottawa River to the Mattawa River to the French River and then to Sault Ste. Marie. **1**

Unable to find the copper deposit, Jolliet resolved to return to Montréal without Peré. He convinced the Ottawa to give him an Iroquois slave as a token of the peace that Governor Courcelle wanted the Ottawa to maintain with the Iroquois. There was a certain irony to Jolliet being given an Iroquois slave as when he was but sixteen years old he had been taken as a captive by the Iroquois and confined, ultimately to be returned to the French. His was a far better fate than many encountered.

Having begun his journey to Lake Superior sometime in 1668, a full year before our travellers, sometime in the spring of 1669 Jolliet had become ill and set upon his return to Montréal. With the melting of the ice in May Jolliet set out for home accompanied by the slave and by another Frenchman who had been paid to make the voyage, a man named La Sotière. **2**

Given his instructions from Courcelle to see if there was a better way to transport minerals to Montréal, Jolliet learned from the Iroquois slave of another route to the east. Separating from his main party Jolliet, La Sotière and the slave canoed south on Lake Huron to the St. Clair River then to Lake St. Clair and the Detroit River. He was the first European to enter Lake Erie at its western end.

It was the Iroquois slave who showed Jolliet this new route which until then was unknown to the French. So it came to pass that even as Dollier and company paddled westward along the south shore of Lake Ontario, at the same time Jolliet was descending the Detroit River (with the current in his favour) and then past Point Pelée. Somewhere well east of Point Pelée, the Iroquois slave convinced Jolliet that further travel by water was not advisable due to the possibility of capture by Andaste's raiding from the south, a tribe that surely would have shown little mercy to the French and even less to the Iroquois.

Jolliet's original plan was to travel by canoe the complete length of the north shore of Lake Erie and then portage around Niagara Falls. It was thus his Iroquois slave who provided Jolliet with the knowledge of the interconnectedness of Erie and Ontario and this was passed on to Galinée. The sound of the Falls which he had heard and the knowledge Galinée had gained at Tinaoutoua, told Galinée that the Niagara River was the "communication" between Lake Erie and Lake Ontario.

The threat of attack by hostile Andastes convinced Jolliet to abandon his canoe, hide it under cover and proceed overland. Had he not done so noted Galinée, Jolliet would have been the first to reach Lake Ontario by this new water route. The three men then proceeded on foot fifty leagues overland (according to Galinée) to a fortuitous meeting with Dollier and La Salle at Tinaoutoua. Jolliet's description to Dollier included news of the location of the Potawatomis (then occupying parts of Michigan and the head waters of the Ohio and Mississippi Rivers) which Nation he said had never seen missionaries. This struck Dollier as an attractive end destination particularly as they would encounter the Algonkian speaking Ottawa's whose language both he and Galinée knew. La Salle's interest in continuing on with the journey began to significantly wane.

As it happened, and once again to the very good fortune of Dollier and company, Jolliet was able to precisely re-count where he had hidden his canoe and told Galinée where they could find it. It was carefully concealed, (according to James Coyne) at a place that would later be known as Port Stanley.

Jolliet and his companions had walked approximately one hundred and fifty miles overland from Port Stanley to Tinaoutoua (or 50 leagues at 3.4 miles to a maritime league, see Endnote 6 for Chapter 8). He detailed his route to Galinée permitting the latter to conceptualize it and create a map for later use as they travelled westward. The map revealed the inter-connectedness of the lakes both from native reports and what Jolliet had seen.

The nervousness or intrigue of Jolliet's guide, which diverted the latter to an overland route would prove in the end to be a life saver for Dollier and Galinée. Galinée made his chart at Tinaoutoua in the "*Naval*" or "*Marine* "fashion as he would describe it, using Jolliet's eastbound route as a guide for the next stage of their travels. This was increasingly necessary because of a falling out with a native who had promised to guide the French onward. A warrior had arrived at Tinaoutoua with some brandy he had obtained from the Dutch. The prospective guide paid for the brandy by selling all the goods Dollier had given him in payment for his future guiding services including a greatcoat. Galinée seized the coat back from the brandy vendor leaving the guide's bill for the brandy unpaid.

The French had no more items left to trade. Armed with Jolliet's detailed information and sans-guide they resolved to push on. Not so La Salle. Galinée noted that before even starting out La Salle…"*had been led to expect that by making some present to the Village of the Senecas he could readily procure slaves of the tribes to which he intended to go, who might serve him as guides.*" This did not transpire at Ganondagan or Tinoutoua. The slave of Nitarkyk did not belong to La Salle. It is never clarified "who" it was that created this expectation in the mind of La Salle, if indeed anyone other than himself, that he could obtain a slave or guide for the next part of the journey.

Lingering at the village with his paid companions until September 30th, La Salle declared his settled intention to return to Montréal. Before La Salle left as had been their practice at least three times a week, Dollier said Mass in the presence of the entire company of Frenchmen. **3**

As an Altar to celebrate Mass, Dollier used canoe paddles resting on forked sticks. Galineé wrote…

"Hitherto we had never failed to hear Holy Mass three times a week, which M. Dollier said for us on a little altar prepared with paddles on forked sticks and surrounded with sails *from our canoes."*

But they did not want the Natives to observe the service.

Surrounding the Frenchman was a curtain made from the sails from the canoes. **4** This extraordinary effort to conceal the ceremony, although inconsistent with their stated purpose of conversion was done to assuage the Sulpician's fear that the Natives would *"perhaps make a mockery of our holy ceremony."* This was somewhat at odds with their stated intention to the Natives of Tinaoutoua to whom they had promised that other Back Robes would come and visit the following year. **5** The Iroquois of Tinaoutoua had requested this perhaps recognizing, like their kinsmen at Kenté that there was a certain protection from French assault provided by the presence of a Priest or two.

If there was any temptation on the part of the seven soldiers to return to Montréal it was not detected by Galinée who noted that *"we had no trouble in persuading our men to follow us."* All seven men still had a high degree of confidence in Père Dollier.

La Salle thus took his leave. He had stated his intention to abandon Dollier's group and he begged their pardon indicating he was returning to Montréal. He would not figure directly any further in the story of our travellers although he would remain a major figure in the life of New France and particularly so after the arrival in 1672 of the new Governor Frontenac. The reader can learn of La Salle's ultimate fate in Chapter Fifteen. He left the Dutchman with Dollier.

Of Adrien Jolliet this much is known. On September 30th Jolliet headed eastward towards home. Just sixty days later, on December 1st Adrien Jolliet died at his home in Cap-de-la-Madeleine, part of modern day Trois Rivières. Jolliet could not have covered that distance on foot with his deteriorating health. It is most likely that he embarked by canoe with La Salle and followed the north shore of Lake Ontario, past present day Toronto and the Kenté Mission (near modern day Consecon, Ontario) thence to Montréal and directly to Cap-de-la-Madelaine. At his death Jolliet was only 27 years old. His swift return home gives us a clue of the route La Salle may have taken back to Montréal.

The Dollier party set out on October 1st, for the banks of the river that would take them to Lake Erie. It took them three days to cover the nine or ten leagues **6** once again travelling through dense forest and with all the impediments associated with portaging, but helped by the Natives even to the point where this time the Natives carried the Frenchmen's precious canoes. They were led to the Grand by a Native of the Chouanons, a Pennsylvania tribe who had been at Tinaoutoua.

They arrived on St. Francis Day, October 3rd and celebrated Mass on the banks of the Grand River. The river… the Grand River…was called the *"Rivière Rapide"* by Galinée as the water flowed with great violence even in October, but over a very shallow depth in places. For the modern reader who has canoed the river in late summer, the feature of sudden gravel bars or other shallows is still a common aspect of navigation on that waterway.

Galinée called the men together and asked who would travel by water and who would go overland to the place where Jolliet had hidden his canoe. La Salle had left them only with their three canoes. It was not possible for twelve men to travel down the river in three canoes given the seasonal shallowness of the river. This democratic kind of consultation with the men would happen again before journey's end. Perhaps it was more than a little than naïve of Galinée and Dollier but the Dutchman offered to go along with the Chouanon who had guided them to the Grand River. The third person to go with them to search for Jolliet's canoe was the slave! This was the same slave of Nitarikyk whose original story had started the entire venture.

As Galinée perceived that the Dutchman was one of the most intelligent of the men (*le plus intelligent*). Galinée reviewed with him the route to the precise location of Jolliet's canoe. The Dutchman asserted that he thoroughly understood the route and that he would find the canoe "without fail" (*infailliblement*). Galinée outfitted the threesome with provisions and ammunition for their weapons. The Dutchman and the Natives then set out on foot to the place of Jolliet's hidden canoe. What is known with complete certainty is that they were never heard from again.

If they made it to the place of the canoe, they did not use it as we shall see. Or they made it there but did not access the canoe which would be unusual. There remain three other possibilities. They perished in wood and all were killed or some were killed. Or all went happily on their separate ways, the Dutchman back to former Dutch territory and the Natives back to their own people. Surely the Dutchman's abilities in the Iroquois language would be of little or no use as the party moved deeper into Ohio territory. The former slave of Nitarikyk, who had travelled on the state sponsored trip heading always towards his homeland must have been smiling to himself as they set out.

The nine remaining Frenchmen would descend the Grand River and travel Lake Erie based on Jolliet's description, and Galinée's map and they would be alone in the wilderness for the first time. Loading as many provisions as possible into the three canoes, and with only two men in each canoe, the party made the descent of the Grand. Three men followed the canoes on the rivers shoreline with all parties stepping frequently into the water to drag the canoes over gravel barriers as the water level was so low.

Descending the river with the current, the journey of approximately forty leagues took them eight full days. Although Etienne Brulé may have descended the Grand some forty years earlier he had left no record of it. They were the first Europeans known to arrive at the mouth of the Grand River at the shore of Lake Erie. They arrived there on October 13th or 14th. Through multiple oxbows and deeply forested banks, the travellers passed down a River that today bisects the City of Brantford, the Six Nations Reserve, the Villages of Cayuga and Dunnville and that ultimately empties into Lake Erie at modern day Port Maitland. What a different view it must have been from todays developed river shoreline.

They had arrived at what Galinée described again as a great sea. All nine men re-entered the canoes. Galinée noted the strong winds that generated large waves due to the Lake's extent (on this he was correct) and its great depth (and here he was in error). The high waves of Lake Erie which are still a feature of the autumn months on the lake speak to the skill of the French to maintain their fragile craft while paddling fully loaded and parallel to the shore.

Initially interpreting the distant Long Point shore as the far shore of the lake, Galinée took careful measurements and identified with some degree of correctness that the north shore of the lake was "*about 42 degrees of latitude*" (He was reasonably accurate with his measurement as the Town of Port Maitland at the mouth of the Grand River is 42.86° North Latitude). But in due course he recognised that the "*far shore*" was in fact a great peninsula (Long Point) which he drew on his map.

Galinée's map would show a grossly inflated Long Point on its axis of width but is roughly correct in its length and in its relationship to the shoreline of Lake Erie. Even so, the modern reader viewing the map should recall that Long Point would look quite different in 1669 compared to the 21st Century as the Point itself is an artifact created by wind, current and erosion. Today, on the clearest of days, from the cliffs to the east of Port Dover the shore line of modern Pennsylvania can "just" be made out visually (see Figure 22 to view part of Galinée's map).

Difficult and incessant paddling finally brought them after three days to the location of their overwintering. On October 17th, 1669, they arrived at "*a spot which appeared to us so beautiful with such an abundance of game, that we thought we could not find a better place in which to pass the winter.*"

They had arrived at what would be known one day as Port Dover in Norfolk County, Ontario. They would spend over five months living in a fortified structure they built, living off the land, living sometimes in fear but comforted by regular celebration of the Mass and well fed with food including wine that they would make themselves.

The reader might imagine a winter's day as Christmas approached, at their camp site with the snow falling about their cabin, with the gentle singing of the Kyrie Eleison, and the voices of the nine men as part of the celebration of the Eucharist, a service that Dollier would regularly perform. Smoke from their encampment, snowshoe tracks in the forest and the sound of their music would reveal their presence.

And from the forest…the Iroquois were watching.

HENRI'S STORY
Seul

It was at the Iroquois village at the head of the lac des Iroquois that M. La Salle announced he would not be travelling any further with us. Our small group of my six comrades wondered why that was but the Holy Fathers told us little only that we should carry on and put our faith in God. We knew that we would be losing many muskets and that we would be travelling alone into the lands that M. Jolliet had told the Holy Fathers about. The Natives took us to a large river that flowed south and it was into its waters we put our canoes. It was late in the season and although one could see that in the Spring the river was possessed of a strong current, in those months the water was not as deep so we were obliged to tow the canoes often over gravel bars or walk in the water beside them.

Eventually the water deepened and we could paddle again arriving at another great inland fresh water sea. Père Galinée told us it was Lac des Chats or Erié named after a tribe known only to the Iroquois. We paddled for several days following the shoreline. This was difficult because the winds blew across our heavily laden canoes and we had to be careful not to capsize. Beforehand the Fathers had sent the Dutchman on with two Natives. We never saw them again. I feared no one would see us again. At last we came to a place where the Fathers said we would stop and build a place to shelter for the winter. Our daily paddling was replaced with the daily use of our axes as we needed a great deal of wood.

The leaves of the forest had started to fall and it was the best time to hunt and smoke as much meat as we could for the coming months. Our work on the water ended for the time but our work on the land began.

We hunted. We went deep into the forest to the north of the lake's shore. We could not go too far as when we were successful in the hunt we had to drag the animals carcass back to the wintering site for cleaning and smoking as no man could survive in the woods at night having spilt the blood of a deer because the many wolves in the area were fearless and would have taken the carcass and us. Thus we never hunted alone. I hunted with my one particular friend Thomàs with who I shared our canoe along with Père Galinée. Our hunts would have failed if we had not left Montréal with the new flintlock musketoons. The burning matchlocks some of the inhabitants still possessed would have betrayed our position to the deer, which although numerous were difficult to shoot except when they came to drink as the forest branches were so dense no clear shot could be had without revealing ourselves. God provided for us. We needed to shoot well so as to not waste our precious gunpowder and shot for if our hunt failed we surely would have suffered for want of food.

It was late in the season when the first snow fell and we prepared our minds and souls for what would be our captivity in this place for the next several months until the arrival of Spring. I felt as though I was in the most remote part of the world.

CHAPTER 9

The Over Wintering of 1669 - 1670 At Port Dover

———

Friday December 13th, 1669

The Wintering Place Port Dover

42.78° North Latitude

80.23° West Longitude

104 days since departure from Montréal

Approximately 896 kilometers from the Island of Montréal

"This earthly paradise of Canada; I call it so because there is assuredly no more beautiful region in all Canada"

JOURNAL OF GALINÉE

TODAY, MOTOR BOATS AND SAIL boats travel out into Lake Erie from the mouth of the Lynn River having passed the length of pier and past the hot dog stands and the Harbour Museum, while thousands of people flock to the beach at Port Dover on a hot summer's day. The busy harbour shelters fishing tugs and large vessels that service the gas wells of Lake Erie. Even on a cold winter day the streets of the Town are busy as people park their cars at the pier and feed the wild birds or watch the ice flows on the Lake. What a different picture it was on a December day in 1669.

A somewhat forlorn sign on Queens Highway #69 to the east of downtown Port Dover marks the wintering site of Dollier and Galinée designated in 1922 as a National Historic Site. After a short drive through a suburb one finds the designated site off Donjon Boulevard (The reader may choose to read Appendix A concerning the designation and precise location of the Wintering Site).

It was near this spot that Dollier built their winter refuge. It was a place to keep warm, to cook, to pray and to defend oneself if need be. As well they stored their precious canoes from the anticipated winter weather. All of this took a lot of work and time was running short before the killing cold of deep winter arrived.

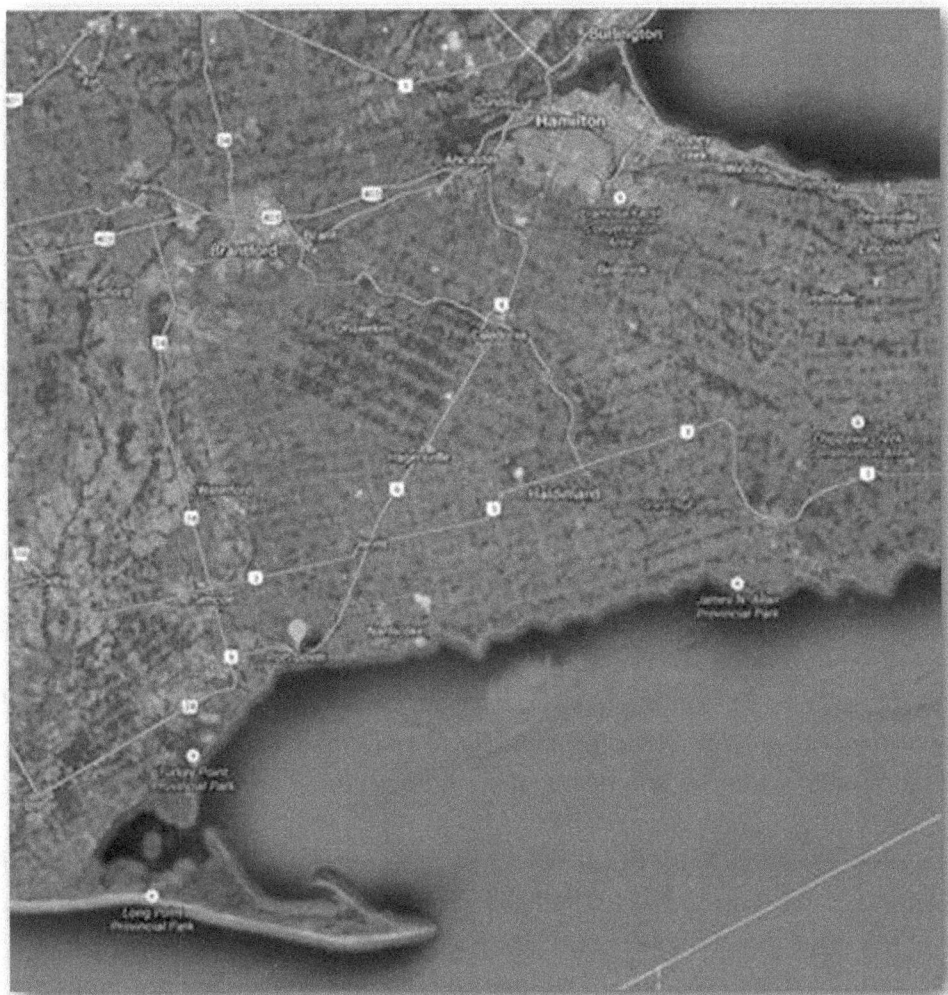

Figure 18. Satellite Google image showing Port Dover Wintering site and
its relation to Long Point Bay and the Inner Bay of Long Point.

It was cold. Yet evidently their clothes and their shelter were sufficient to protect them as Galinée would make no complaints of frostbite, injury or other physical ailment upon their ultimate departure in the Spring. He did note that the winter was severe but that snowfall was light at a mere one foot compared with three feet of snow at Montréal.

"I believe we should have died of cold if we had been in a place where the weather was as severe as Montréal."

There would have been silence broken only by the winds coming off Lake Erie onto the land and disturbing the tree tops. The cold Galinée wrote about was so severe that almost all the axes would break when employed to chop trees for construction of their shelter or for fires. Multiple axes were broken after the January deep freeze set in. **1**

It is likely that the party had snowshoes, or *"racquets"* as the French called them even though there is but one specific and admiring mention of this Native invention in the Journal. The experience of Dollier and the shared knowledge of the seven soldiers of the disastrous French attempt in 1666 against the Iroquois would have informed them fully of the need to have snowshoes in order to penetrate into the forest to hunt and collect wood. Only some of the men of that earlier ill-fated expedition had snow shoes and fewer still of the regular French soldiers (unlike the Canadiens) knew how to use them.

Immediately upon arrival and before major work on the winter habitation commenced, Dollier had sent two of the men to the place where Jolliet had hidden the canoe. To that end they must have been well briefed by Galinée. They returned in a week and said they had found the canoe, a tribute to Jolliet's accuracy. But they also reported that there was no sign of the Dutchman or the two Natives. Having been gone a week it is most likely the two men would have travelled by canoe. Assuming this is so and that they followed the shoreline described by Jolliet they must have portaged across the neck of Long Point and thereby given Dollier some idea of what route they would encounter in the Spring.

The absence of the Dutchman and his companions troubled Dollier *"extremely"* but there was nothing to do but construct their winter habitation and see if the others turned up.

Their daily concern had to be the preservation of their canoes. It is implicit that they sheltered the canoes with the materials at hand. The canoes were their lifeline to carry on with their Mission and to return to Montréal. There would be no tree sap to repair them until late Spring except for that which had been stored. The local trees would not provide the appropriate bark or wood to effect repairs at that later time of year. Where did this ability to adapt and survive in the woods originate from?

It came from Dollier. The reader of Galinées Journal will recall that the opening Chapters of this work reference the fact that Dollier spent part of the Winter of 1669 in the Territory of the Nipissing in order to learn their language. He must have also learned something of their techniques and skills needed for winter. Even before that time he had seen firsthand what was required for winter survival during the disastrous Courcelle expedition of 1666. Therefore Dollier had more experience than many Frenchmen and likely more than all others in his party or LaSalle's. Dollier would understand the need to act on his knowledge, after all he had been an Cavalry Officer serving in the field of battle in Europe.

Jolliet would have impressed on Dollier the preference of travel by water compared with his excruciating overland trek. An overland trip back to Montréal was unthinkable. The canoes meant everything to the expedition and this speaks to the issue of where the wintering site would have been located.

The Journal speaks of the success they had in hunting and that they stored their provisions in a *"magazin"* or granary. This had to be of sufficient size to store the animals they killed yet close enough to protect them from wandering wolves or bears who had failed to hibernate...and both were plentiful in the area at the time. To that end and for accommodation and defence they constructed a cabin that was built large enough for the nine men but that could also be defended. Its construction was a matter of some pride on the part of Galinée who observed that had they been attacked by marauding Iroquois *"...we could have defended ourselves for a long time."*

The habitation was large enough then for nine men and all their provisions. The granary was close to their cabin or part of it. The cabin must also have had a fire pit of sorts for cooking and warmth yet with a vent designed to permit the escape of smoke. Many First Nation Longhouses lacked any air vents with the result that the occupants would develop respiratory issues in the winter, some of which would attenuate only in the Spring when warmer temperatures permitted outdoor movement. The Cabin and any other structures would have been built without nails. Nails weighed far too much and would not have been transportable in the canoes. The only mention of casks in the Journal is a reference to small casks of gunpowder, which along with the necessary, shot and powder would be as carefully tended to as the canoes and the paddles.

In brief, the structure must have been of some reasonable size. With hunting activity taking place, the sound of shooting in the forest and smoke from their fires for warmth and smoking of meat it might have been anticipated that they would be discovered in time by roving parties of Iroquois. And so they were.

Early in the New Year, a hunting party of Iroquois came upon the French and spoke with them at the wintering site. The exchange, linguistic barriers aside according to Galinée, was sufficient for the Natives to express their admiration of the French building efforts and to return later, on a number of occasions with other Natives to see it as well. The other possibility is that the Natives came to inspect not the cabin but to inspect the French and to send word back where they were and what they were doing. The French resolve and zeal for their Mission would have been evident.

And the source of this resolve …this zèle, what was the passion that kept these men going? Their 'zeal' came from their faith. Galinée relates that…

"We erected a pretty altar at the end of our cabin where we had the happiness to hear Holy Mass three times a week without missing, with the consolation you may imagine of finding ourselves with our good God, in the midst of the woods, in a land where no European had ever been. Monsieur Dollier often told us that the winter ought to be worth to us, as regards our eternal welfare, more than the best ten years of our life. We confessed often, received communion as well… In short we had our parochial mass, holidays and Sundays, with the necessary instructions; prayer evening and morning and every other Christian exercise. Orison was offered with tranquility in the middle of this solitude, where we saw no stranger for three months."

And they had wine.

Galinée took care to provide the reader of his Journal with great detail on certain culinary points. Among those detailed descriptions was the group's finding that at Port Dover, in addition to apples, plums, walnuts and chestnuts for their granary, there grew wild grapes. *Vitis Riparia* is a wild grape that grows on the river banks of Southern Ontario's forests. Jacques Cartier had observed the grape on the Isle D'Orléans during his voyage in 1534 and was poised to name the Island *"Isle de Bacchus"* but settled on the more politically correct name of a French Royal. Concerning the grapes from which they made the wine, Galinée observed…

" I will tell you, by the way, that the vine grows here only in sand, on the banks of lakes and river, but although it has no cultivation it does not fail to produce grapes in great quantities as large and as sweet as the finest of France. We even made wine of them, with which M. Dollier said Holy Mass all winter, and it was as good as vin de Grave. It was a heavy dark wine like the latter. Only red grapes are seen here, but in so great quantities, that we found places where one could easily have made 25 or 30 barriques of wine." **2**

The Vin de Grave wine Galinée referred to is cultivated in the Graves Region near Bordeaux, a City on the Garonne River in France. Wines from the Bordeaux Region including Vins de Graves were imported from France to Québec in great quantity by 1669 (see LaFrance M. bibliography). **3**

The glacial sand plains of Norfolk County had delivered a veritable food basket for the French. With hunting and smoking of meat, preparation of stores and the preservation of the canoes and the construction of the cabin, their early days on the site before the onset of the deep January cold must have been full of activity. Wood had to be chopped for all of their shelters and structures. More wood had to be chopped daily for their fires. It is unlikely that had any of the party remained in Montréal would they have had such a healthy diet and environment, however socially isolating from others it may have been in the wilderness.

The area had an abundance of fish, beaver, and ample deer. In addition the mild early winter led to the successful hunt for bears which Galinée said were *"fatter and of better flavour than the most savoury pigs of France."*

Deliberately or not, the inclusion of apples, plums and red wine in their diet would have provided them with essential vitamin C. There would be no reports of the onset of scurvy. This alone was an amazing fact perhaps borne of Dollier's experience in the 1666 expedition when he cared for soldiers suffering from the debilitating effects of scurvy.

Had any individual on the voyage been so afflicted, they would have become useless as hunters and paddlers until and only if they sufficiently recovered. Of this more will be said in the next Chapter.

As Spring approached the days grew longer and the thought of departure was planted in their minds. Pressing on deeper into the unknown was their principal wish. They did not know that they were about to embark on the most difficult and disheartening part of the voyage. By March of 1670 the time of their departure was nigh. Mass was said and hymns were sung, and their zeal for their mission remained unabated. That would change. Near Starvation and miserable conditions awaited that would bring them close to death.

A disaster lay just ahead that would alter the course of their entire mission.

Henri's Story
L'Hivernement

We would not have survived the winter except for the bounty of the land and the wisdom of Père Dollier. We found a place to spend the dark winter months with good flowing water and where we could store our canoes in a small valley near the river. We built our cabin edge of the hill overlooking the valley so as to be on guard and so as to be able to always protect our canoes.

Our axes broke when we chopped wood. Maybe it was the cold. Maybe it was the axe. But we needed wood for all things, for the cabin and granary and for the strong shelter for our canoes. We needed wood for fire and warmth and cooking. It was endless daily work as the fire could never go out.

As the days got shorter and the weather colder we had to rely on what we had killed and smoked or gathered. I remember sitting in the woods, ever so quietly, concealed and waiting for game. We were surrounded by such silence as I have never encountered. The trees were like giants and reached far into the sky. They reminded me then and even now of the great columns of the cathedral of Rouen which I have seen with my own eyes. The columns of the forest were the columns of God and not of man...and I felt very small.

Father was good to us and would give us some of the wine we had made always saving enough for Holy Mass. The warmth of the wine made up for storing it in the bladders of the deer we had killed but we found we could wash the bladders in the river so that any remaining blood merged with the red wine. Some Iroquois found us in the new year when we were hunting. They brought others to see our cabin. Père Galinée thought they were impressed with our cabin. I told him that I did not believe the Indians came in the deep cold of winter by chance and that I believed they had been sent by the Seneca of the great village or from Tinaoutoua to see what we were doing. Père Galinée told me to put my faith in God. When the winter ended and it was time to leave, we had almost exhausted all of our stored and smoked provisions. We had fared well until then and knew that God would place us under his protection.

CHAPTER 10

Food and Provisions

———

"(The traveller) should not be dainty about eating or drinking, adapting himself to the localities in which he finds himself."

SAMUEL DE CHAMPLAIN 1632 TREATISE ON SEAMANSHIP

" I can assure you…that a person must add the constant fear of dying of hunger or disease in the midst of the forest, without any help."

JOURNAL OF RENÉ DE BRÉHANT DE GALINÉE 1670

FOOD, AND PLENTY OF IT was what fueled the men who propelled the Canoes. For the distances travelled and the work to be done each of the men would require enormous daily caloric intake. And without the balanced diet that the woods and lakes could provide the threat of scurvy would remain. How then did they do it and at the risk of spoiling the end of this narrative, how is it that they all survived? There must have been very detailed planning. With the decision was first taken to make the journey the first thing Dollier did was to travel to Québec.

"With this purpose in view M. Dollier returned from the woods in advance of the Indians with whom he was sojourning, in order to go to Québec to buy the necessary supplies for the undertaking."

Galinée noted that he had but a brief time to prepare but that *"everyone had done* (their own) *packing."* Centralised direction must have occurred because the voyage demonstrated an emphasis on packing provisions with redundancy. If one axe broke while being used for chopping down a tree, there was always another one available.

From the modern perspective the foresight they demonstrated in packing the required correct provisions is impressive save in one particular and important respect as we shall see. Dollier needed to ensure that they had what they needed for the forthcoming seasons. At the time only Dollier is known to have had deep practical training in surviving the winter weather.

The three canoes were only so big. There was a finite amount of cubic space for what was needed while leaving sufficient freeboard for the safe paddling of the canoes. Everything that was absolutely necessary had to be packed but how was one to know what was unnecessary? For the soft items, Galinée described that their packs contained blankets and any winter clothing they would require. He mentions a "small" bag of clothing belonging to one of the men. The packs would have to be secure in the canoes, but of a size that they could be removed when the men came ashore at night and also so that the packs could be carried over whatever portages they might encounter. Dollier and perhaps some of the soldiers had experience with portages and would know of the labour they would entail. At the beginning of the journey, Galinée was largely a novice in every aspect of travel in Canada.

The Twenty First Century reader might consider the following. In order to eat one had to hunt. To hunt meant that they required guns with flints, lead for shot and irreplaceable gunpowder. The latter appears to have been kept in small casks which also had to fit into the canoes. And they needed sufficient quantity of these necessities to hunt the entire winter of 1669 and 1670.

The case suggesting they had flintlock muskets as *Henri* has avered to is circumstantial but compelling. Flintlock weapons were relatively new and expensive but the Sulpicians were very well funded and could afford them. Since they were but a small number of men it is likely that Courcelle would have had no objection to a few of them leaving Montréal. The Carignan-Salières Regiment had in fact received orders, partially ignored, that the flintlocks newly issued to the Regiment in 1665 were to be sent back to France with older weapons to be used by the Garrison.

Galinée makes mention of a gift to the Seneca in upstate New York of a double barrelled pistol which only existed as a flintlock. Galinée describes the recovery of some nearly lost items at Point Pelée as including a "musketoon." Finally their success at hunting suggests the more modern technology of a flintlock. True flintlock arms (as opposed to the snaphaunce, matchlocks or wheel-locks) were recorded in New France as early as the 1630's. For the inhabitants of New France, flintlock arms could be acquired by purchase by the mid 1660's. 1

They fished as well as hunted. Catfish from the St. Lawrence were described as succulent and later, in other parts of the Great Lakes, they had access to great quantities of very nourishing Whitefish. They needed kettles in sufficient number and size to feed all nine men. Galinée mentions that they gave away as gifts no fewer than eleven kettles to the Seneca as well as twelve hatchets, four dozen knives, five or six pounds of glass beads and a two coats. And yet they still had enough axes and knives for their own use to clean the carcasses of the deer, moose and bear that they would kill and eat on their voyage. Again it must be recognized that of the sum total of gifts given to the Natives some would have come from La Salle's provisions.

The loss of even one canoe would mean that they still had some essentials but insufficient space for all the men to paddle. Finally, they needed spare paddles and the right wood and gum material to affect any repairs to the canoes. All of the men travelled with the knowledge they may yet starve if they did not drown in overloaded canoes.

The change of diet upon departure from Montréal made several of them ill in the first days ascending the St. Lawrence. Indian corn or Sagamite would become an important staple of their diet supplemented often by the Natives at the Seneca village, at Tinaoutoua and even what they could carry with them upon departing from Port Dover. Concerning Sagamite, Galinée wrote…*"The ordinary diet is Indian corn, called in France Turkey wheat, which is ground between two stones and boiled in water; the seasoning is with meat or fish, when you have any."*

Early in the journey while still on the St. Lawrence, the travelers shot two moose. Meat that they couldn't eat in the short term they proceeded to smoke when possible as the summer heat rapidly spoiled the fresh meat. Galinée attributed this early wastage to their *"little experience"* at that point. The process obviously took time for cleaning the animal, cutting the necessary amount of wood and smoking the meat. It was a food preservation process they would use from time to time and use most effectively over the winter at Port Dover. Galinée gave a detailed description of the smoking technique.

"The mode of curing it in the woods, where there is no salt, is to cut it in very thin slices and spread it on a gridiron raised three feet from the ground, covered with small wooden switches on which you spread your meat. Then a fire is made underneath the gridiron, and the meat is dried in the fire and smoke until there is no longer any moisture in

it and it is as dry as a piece of wood. It is put up in packages of thirty or forty, rolled up in pieces of bark, and thus wrapped up it will keep five or six years without spoiling. When you wish to eat it you reduce it to powder between two stones and make a broth by boiling with Indian corn."

Hunting and smoking meat took time and that was one commodity that was fixed. At the Seneca village they were offered dog by their hosts and by Galinée's own account, however put off he was by the idea, he ate it. They did decline several portions of human flesh offered to them by the Iroquois from the unfortunate captive the Iroquois had killed. Writing for those in France and those in New France, Galinée described their diet at Port Dover as including from time to time the fish and smoked meat of deer, moose, beaver, wolf and his apparent favourite...bear.

"The woods are open, interspersed with beautiful meadows, watered by rivers and rivulets filled with fish and beaver, an abundance of fruits, and what is more important, so full of game that we saw there at one time more than a hundred roebucks in a single band, herds of fifty or sixty hinds, and bears fatter and of better flavor than the most savory pigs of France. In short, we may say that we passed the winter more comfortably than we should have done in Montréal."

Clearly, amongst the seven men, some or all had the skill to clean the carcass of very large animals. The dilemma was that the forest larder did not consistently provide for their ongoing needs given seasonal changes. Wisely putting aside the smoked meat they had prepared they passed a relatively agreeable winter of 1669-1670 in the forest. Their relative success in hunting suggests that the seven men accompanying the two priests were more experienced than those of La Salle's party. Fear of starvation had been one of the reasons attributed to La Salle in abandoning his companions as Galinée noted in writing of their earlier separation at Tinaoutoua that...

"He (LaSalle) begged us to excuse him if he abandoned us to return to Montréal, and added that he could not make up his mind to winter in the woods with his men, where their lack of skill and experience might make them die of starvation."

There was another factor in their good health over the winter of 1669- 1670. They avoided scurvy. Scurvy is a disease resulting from a lack of vitamin C. It had plagued Jacques Cartier during his first winter at Québec until local Iroquois showed him how to brew a drink from the white cedar that prevents the onset of the condition. Unchecked, the disease would cause weakness and swelling of joints, loosening of teeth in the gums until they fell out and lassitude and weakness that would lead to death. As a mariner Champlain was very familiar with the disease and its effects and although he did not have the native recipe Cartier had, it was generally well known by his era that fresh food was in some unknown way the solution to the condition.

As late as the 1740's the British Admiral Anson circumnavigating the Globe would lose hundreds of his sailors to the scourge of scurvy. In fairness Admiral Anson also had several hundred men crammed into a ship with limited fresh water and virtually no "fresh" foods. Dollier's expedition had at least in 1669, an abundance of both. It may have also been a factor that the Doller party was really quite small and there was little risk of over hunting an area where there was game. This was a circumstance the French had not experienced in 1666 during the Iroquois war when it was impossible to keep over a thousand men adequately fed in the forests of the Richelieu River valley.

On a more terrestrial setting than Admiral Anson was the future experience of the French, when in 1687 after having attacked the Seneca the French built a small fort at the mouth of the Niagara River where Fort Niagara is now located. The French left one hundred men with their salt-preserved provisions to spend the winter there. When a relief ship crossed Lake Ontario in the spring of 1688 to Niagara, only twelve men were left alive, the remaining eighty-eight having died of scurvy. They had plenty of food to eat, just not the right kind of food.

Dollier and Galinée had access to fruit. They had access to grapes. As Frenchmen in the wilderness they made wine for use in the Mass but also for their general consumption and thus had their protection from scurvy. Galinée wrote…

"…we awaited the winter with tranquility whilst hunting and making good provision of walnuts and chestnuts, which were there in great quantities. We had indeed in our granary 23 or 24 minots of these fruits, besides apples, plums and grapes, and alizes of which we had an abundance during the autumn."

At Port Dover they experienced what Galinée called *"the earthly paradise of Canada."* He further wrote …

"The moment we arrived we killed a stag and a hind, and again on the following day two young stags. The good hunting quite determined us to remain in this place. We looked for some favorable spot to make a winter camp, and discovered a very pretty river, at the mouth of which we camped."

How was it that Dollier's party had the knowledge concerning food that would see them through? The answer lies again in the past personal experiences of Dollier. As noted in two previous Chapters, Dollier had firsthand experience of the effect of winter on men in the forest. When Dollier was tasked with leading the aide party to Fort Ste. Anne in 1666 this was his first training school for winter travel and survival in Canada.

Dollier's further schooling in winter survival came in the winter of 1668-1669 when he had travelled to the land of the Nipissing for the specific purpose of learning their language. He would have seen how the First Nations survived in the frigid climate. They were his tutors in language and in winter survival. The knowledge that went this experience included knowledge of clothing, food and no doubt snowshoes. His knowledge of winter and travel necessities were thus current and fresh in mind.

Finally Dollier, was armed with a keen sense of situational awareness and would have learned from others (perhaps such as the Jesuit Chaumonot) who had passed many winters in New France and Canada. Dollier was not one to believe that winter travel in Canada was anything like his experiences in France. Dollier followed the wise counsel of Champlain himself, quoted at the opening of this Chapter, that is to say he adapted himself *to the localities in which he (found) himself,* and caused his companions to do the same. The days at the wintering site were their halcyon days with respect to the abundance and variety of food.

Spring has always been a time of want for early explorers. Spring was the time of worst famine for peasants in Europe. The harvested supplies of the previous year, so carefully hoarded over the winter would have been exhausted. By February and March of 1670, there would be no nuts or fruit nor a domestic harvest available to Dollier. The deer would have retreated deep into the forest to eat bark or what few tree shoots remained and in any event, with the melting snows not only would tracking and hunting be much more difficult, the forest would become almost impassable in the muck.

Spring, for many reasons, meant it was time to move on and soon after their departure from Port Dover they would encounter deep misery and their own time of near starvation.

CHAPTER 11

Exodus: Spring 1670

Port Stanley; Rivière Tonti

42.78° North Latitude

81.23° West Longitude

Approximately 990 kilometers from Island of Montréal

280 Days since departure from Montréal

Approximately 94 kilometers and 16 days from Wintering Site

*"We had no provisions left, and M. Dollier and myself had deprived ourselves of part of our
share to give to our men, so that they might have more strength to go hunting."*

JOURNAL OF GALINÉE SPRING 1670

THE VILLAGE OF PORT STANLEY, Ontario whose estimated population in 2015 was two thousand souls, is situated on the north shore of Lake Erie. The village is bisected by Kettle Creek on which can be found pleasure craft and some fishing vessels that still ply the commercial fisheries of Lake Erie. In the summer time the village population, like that of Port Dover swells to many thousands if not tens of thousands as city dwellers from London, Ontario and elsewhere are drawn to its beaches.

Inscribed on a plaque on a stone cairn at the main intersection of the Village is a reference to Dollier and Gallinée. It says in part...

"Kettle Creek was called by the Iroquois the "Kanagio", by the Ojibwas the "Akiksibi", by the French the "Rivière Tonti". Among early visitors were: Louis Jolliet, September,1669; Dollier and Galinée, April 1670."

Was it here that Dollier found the canoe left for him based on the information Adrien Jolliet had provided and the Chart prepared by Galinée? James Coyne in his 1903 study asserted that it was "probably" so, but perhaps not. The statement on the Port Stanley Cairn asserting that it was Louis Jolliet has to be compared with the correct comment found on an Ontario Historical Plaque, at the aptly named La Salle Park at the City of Burlington, Ontario. The latter states that our party of travellers met with Adrien Jolliet. Other sources make it certain that this was so.

Conflicting cairns of the Twentieth Century aside, where had Adrien Jolliet hidden his canoe? Was it even at Port Stanley? There are some clues that raise other possibilities. Upon arrival at the site of the wintering place in September 1669, Dollier had dispatched two of the men to the *place of the canoe* as described so carefully by Jolliet. The men returned at the end of a week and advised that based on the Jolliet description, they had found it but had seen no sign of the Dutchman or his two native companions.

The Galinée text says that the men returned *"après huit jours"*, or after eight days. From the wintering site at Port Dover to Port Stanley is a distance by land of approximately one hundred kilometers. Assuming that there was a native trail following the shoreline (and the existence of such a trail was well documented by the late Eighteenth Century) they would have had to travel twenty-five kilometers a day at a time of waning daylight to find the concealed canoe and then return. Their brief reconnaissance mission would provide Dollier with some information as to what he would encounter in the following Spring.

Galinée's map is lacking in details here other than noting the meadows on the north shore of Lake Erie to the West of the neck of Long Point. It is possible that the canoe was hidden by Jolliet either at Port Burwell, approximately sixty kilometers from the Wintering Site or even Port Bruce. The former site however is marked by a very deep ravine cut by Big Otter Creek with meadows above the ravine. This would be a good place to hide a canoe and preserve it from the elements. Galinée's map does depict four roughly equal streams running south into the lake so that the precise location may never be known. What is certain is that Dollier and company at the very least would have ultimately passed through Port Stanley. Rivière Tonti as referred to on the Cairn was named by the French after a close companion of La Salle's who would also pass through Port Stanley, but several years later. **1**

Previously, over the five and half months of overwintering, the party had longed for the Spring navigation season to begin. It was at this point in the Journal that Galinée explained their haste to get moving. Dollier would not be returning to New France. He was going to act on his earlier resolution to remain in the Ohio country. Upon reaching the land of the Potawatomis it was Galinée's intention to return to Montréal that calendar year and then to return to Dollier with what he would require for his proselytizing mission.

On Sunday March 23rd 1670, having resolved to set out on Wednesday the 26th (the day after the Feast of the Annunciation) the French left their cabin for the shore line of Lake Erie, there to engage in the simple act of planting a Cross and offering their prayers. But it was to be much more than just that.

On the edge of the lake a Cross was planted (see Appendix A concerning the location of the modern commemorative Cross marker) which most people would perceive as a religious act performed by these devout men. It was also a political act of the greatest importance to Colbert and Louis XIV in France. In raising the Cross they attached a copy of the Coat of Arms of France made of wood along with a placard at its base. The priests read out the words on the placard and claimed the land for France. **2** Memorialized in writing in what is known as the *procès-vérbal* or memorandum (which repeated the words on the placard) the Sulpicians claimed the land for France. Why were the priests engaged in a political act of this magnitude?

The words they appended to the Cross and copied into the written *procès-verbal* were as follows...

" We, the undersigned, certify that we have seen, on the lands of the lake named Erie, the arms of the king of France attached to the foot of a cross, with this inscription: The year of salvation 1669, Clement IX, being seated in the chair of St. Peter, Louis XIV, reigning in France, Monsieur de Courcelle being governor of New France, and Monsieur Talon being Intendant therein for the King, there arrived in this place two missionaries, of the Seminary of Montréal, accompanied by seven other Frenchmen, who the first of all European people have wintered on this lake, of which they have taken possession in the name of their King, as of an unoccupied territory, by affixing his arms which they have attached here to the foot of this Cross' In testimony whereof we have signed the present certificate. **3**
Signed
Francois Dollier, Priest of the Diocese of Nantes, in Brittany.
De Galinée, Deacon of the Diocese of Rennes, in Brittany."

Needless to say, the Natives were not consulted. Although with the departure of the French, the land would essentially be "unoccupied" once again. This Procès-Vérbal was not addressed to the Natives. It was addressed to the King and Government of France. But it was written for the English and any remnant Dutch in upstate New York. It was the equivalent of a trespass notice so that the French could operate in the Region and claim priority over any annoying English who might press northward. This was European dynastic politics at play in the forests of the New World.

The Order to take possession of the lands clearly had come from their secular superiors, that is to say Courcelle, who unlike the Intendant Talon, was alone responsible for such political actions. The French Government did not expect the Cross and Declaration posted on the Cross to stay there for long. Their real intentions were revealed in a subsequent letter dated November 10th, 1670 from Intendant Jean Talon to be read by Minister Colbert to no less a person than the King, Louis XIV wherein he stated…

*" I return now to the new discoveries, and I say that already MM. Dollier and Galinée, priests of Saint-Sulpice, missionaries at Montréal, have travelled through Lake Ontario and visited unknown nations; the map which I have appended hereto, under the letter C, will show their route and how far they have penetrated…The small minute marked D, which they drew up a little hastily and without giving it proper form, will give you some evidence that they have taken possession of all that area….***I am assured that the practice of the Iroquois is to pull down the arms and written placards which are attached to the trees of the places of which possession is being taken, and to take them to the English***.(author's emphasis) Thus this nation may learn that we intend to remain masters thereof."* (Source, *French Regime in the Upper Country* p. 66 citing Margry).

Jean Talon (1626-1694), Intendant of New France had in fact left for France at this time but would return shortly thereafter to Canada. Talon's assurance that the Iroquois would inevitably tear down the placard attached to the Cross likely arose from the experience of Courcelle and his military commander Alexandre de Prouville de Tracy in the 1666 war against the Iroquois when after destroying the villages and foodstuffs of the Mohawks they executed a similar claim of land in upstate New York by raising a Cross with the Royal Arms attached and with a similar declaration of sovereignty. It is likely that Tracey's earlier placard had reached the English in Albany and word of same had reached Courcelle. The Natives were meant to be the carriers of Dollier's placard to the English so they would know that the French had laid first claim to the lands of what is now southern Ontario. It was in effect a "postcard" sent from Port Dover by the French addressed to the English. Simply put it stated "We were here first, stay out!"

Figure 19 Text of the *Procès-verbal* or memoranda in Dollier's handwriting claiming the wintering site for France. The unfortunate stamp on this original document of the *Archives Coloniales*, is modern. The document rests in the National Library of France.

It might be observed as well that the claim to possess the lands was a claim of sovereignty over the land to the exclusion of the English and that it was not a claim of adverse possession over the Natives. Previously in 1665 Louis XIV had instructed Courcelle that although French policy was to convert the Natives to Christianity and to have them as his subjects, occupation of their lands was not part of French policy. That would change later. Indeed, other than enclaves where agriculture was established to maintain small post, (such as Detroit in 1701) most French Forts and posts of the era were built for the purpose of having the Natives bring furs to the French. The un-licenced Coureurs de Bois sought to upset this trading model by going themselves to the source of the furs as it were and hence were outside of the law.

The far more populous English colonies took a different approach which was to displace the Natives for the purpose of settlement. By 1759 the population differences became enormous with over two million English colonists inhabiting the thirteen colonies versus sixty thousand European inhabitants for all of New France. The French under Louis XIV's senior Minister Jean Colbert wanted conversions to Catholicism and profit from furs for France and not much else unless there were to be large profits with little investment.

Jean Baptiste Colbert (1619-1683), the man to whom Talon wrote, was the Minister of Finance and Marine under Louis XIV. Next only to the King he was the most powerful man at Court. Left alone Colbert might have brought France, the most populous country in Europe to greater heights of achievement but he despaired constantly over Louis XIV's huge expenditures on his armies and his wars and then after 1670, there was more financial despair over the massive construction of the Palace of Versailles. All Intendants in France and in Colonies reported to Colbert. He had an extensive intelligence network from which he passed on information to the King through various secretaries. It was thus to Colbert that Talon would write of Dollier and Galinée's actions knowing that the King would be fully informed of the letter's contents. If Louis XIV basked for a while during his reign in glory and held the admiration of his people, Colbert the politician was identified by the common people with the dreaded tax gatherers of France. When he died there was general rejoicing and he was buried at night to avoid riots breaking out.

Talon closed his letter to Colbert and the King by asking if this *"procédure"* of laying claim to the land with a view to shutting out the English should be continued or stopped. The answer that he must have been received from Louis XIV is made apparent in the direction Talon gave to subsequent explorers sent to Lake Huron and Lake Superior in 1671. Upon their arrival at Sault Ste. Marie in that June of that year specific "Orders" had been given to similarly lay claim to the land, and erect a cross bearing the Kings Arms. Dollier's actions set the precedent. The raising of the Cross and the reading out of a text similar to the Procès-Verbal would be the procedure that all New France would follow across what is now Canada and deep into the United States.

The importance of the Procès-Verbal would be evidenced by the written document completed in the handwriting of Dollier himself (see Figure 19 above) and which was forwarded under separate cover directly to France upon its receipt by Governor Courcelle in the Autumn of 1670.

Perceiving that Lake Erie "appeared" to be clear of ice, even though their river Black Creek (also known sometimes as Patterson's Creek) was not, the French portaged all of their effects to the edge of the lake, leaving their cabin to the elements and thus they set out once more after five and half months of over wintering. It was March 26th, 1670 and just as they had begun their journey months before in Montréal with the first stoke of their paddles, so once again they pushed into the open water of Lake Erie and turned west with their next landfall in the vicinity of the modern town of Port Rowan at the neck of the great sand peninsula of Long Point.

To arrive at Long Point they needed to pass the marshlands that extend out into the lake on the Inner Bay of Long Point and this proved problematic. Then as now, late Winter and early Spring winds off Lake Erie often blow ice into the Inner Bay of the Point. The southerly winds would also have made paddling parallel to the shore a perilous experience with the minimal freeboard they had between the edge of their canoes and the water. They headed west towards the juncture of Long Point and the mainland.

As briefly commented upon earlier in Chapter Two, it might be said that there are two Lake Eries. The smaller Lake Erie is that large body of water "inside" Long Point, the latter being approximately thirty-five kilometers long and with its tip some thirty kilometers off shore from Port Dover. It is the largest Fresh Water Sand Peninsula in the World and no doubt had somewhat different dimensions three hundred and fifty years ago. Today lake freighters often take shelter from poor weather and from the dangers of the open lake inside Long Point, meaning the "second" Lake Erie. The two bodies of water, the inside aspect of Long Point and further its "Inner" Bay when compared to the waters outside, or on the south and west of Long Point, have very different temperaments. This may account for what Champlain depicted on the map he produced in 1632, his *"Carte de la Nouvelle France"* (see Figure 5) based on Native verbal descriptions where he showed Lake Erie as two separate smaller lakes. It is not a totally inaccurate cartographic "metaphor." French maps made after 1670 would even go so far as to label the Inner Bay of Long Pont as *petit Lac Erié*, or little Lake Erie as did Galinée.

It took two days to cover the distance from Port Dover to Turkey Point, a span that should have taken but one day in better conditions. Then an offshore wind struck. Having paused briefly on the shore due to the weather, a strong wind carried Galinée's insecurely moored canoe out into the lake. Quick action by two of the men enabled them to grapple with the wayward canoe from their own while several hundred metres out in the lake but the strong winds forced them to cut the line to save themselves from drowning. Watching from shore, Galinée saw their attempt had failed and placed himself in one of the two remaining canoes and set out to retrieve his vessel. He too failed and the canoe fully loaded with baggage drifted away into the Inner Bay and out of sight.

The expedition was now reduced to two canoes for the nine men and Dollier's canoe was very heavily loaded. The prospect of rough waters, both literally and figuratively lay ahead. Galinée wrote "*so there we were, consulting what we should do.*" It may be that this inclusive language correctly suggests that the "consultation" once again included the seven men. If there was a dissenting viewpoint on what followed it is not recorded. As events would unfold though, this would not be the last time a failure to secure canoes or baggage would profoundly affect their course of action.

The party moved on. By removing one man from each of the two remaining canoes and filling the space with what remained of Galinée's baggage, four men would continue paddling the canoes and five others, Dollier and Galinée included, would travel by land. If necessary this mode of travel would continue to the place where Jolliet's canoe was hidden and for which Galinée had his map based on the latter's verbal descriptions. Four men in two canoes would travel on an unknown and angry lake, and five men by land on the shore to a destination with the hope that they could locate once more the hidden "Jolliet" canoe. It all painted a scenario of resolve and great risk. But that risk would have to be taken. If Galinée had described their condition months before in ascending the St Lawrence as "*misérable*" he now called it "wretched" (*vilain*).

They had to cross four swollen streams. 4 Galinée called them *rivières*. Another "Council" was held among the five men to discuss how to find a place where the creeks were narrower and hence would be easier to cross before trying to traverse the tree choked and swollen ravines. Although heavily laden with provisions, firearms, ammunition and powder and with only blankets to secure their comfort at night the party of five men travelling by land went north some kilometers in an effort to make their task easier and then struck west, realizing that they would have to regain the shoreline of Lake Erie where it commenced to the west of Long Point.

Even today at these locations Norfolk County is still heavily forested. The original forests of 1670 were even more dense than now. Galinée complained about the density of the woods and the obstructions they encountered. It is the density of the forest that blocks the sunlight so that some of the last snows to vanish when the warm weather returns, is on the forest floor and the very last snows to melt are those found in the valleys of the four creeks that flow south to the Lake. The creek valleys are almost impenetrable until late Spring. Even with the arrival of warm weather fallen trees, deep remnant snow and ice remain in very steeply sided ravines. This is true today. It was also true in late March 1670 when warm weather lay weeks ahead.

When they finally turned west it was only to encounter swamp in the area known today as South Walsingham. The decision was made to cross what was likely Big Creek and they decided to build a raft to do so. Moving somewhat more southerly on the east bank of the creek, about six kilometers from its mouth, they spent the night. Where and how the four men in the canoes passed the night is unknown.

It was that night, Galinée recorded and revealed a mystical aspect of the men's beliefs. They heard voices in the night. Thinking it was perhaps their canoe-bound men calling to them they rushed to the edge of the creek and still heard "*voices*" from the south and the west simultaneously. Galinée attributed this deception to "the Hunting of Arthur "… *la chasse artus*. Founded in early Frankish myth and very much part of belief in 17th Century France, this mystical phenomenon was akin to the Québec saga of *La Chasse Galerie*, wherein hunters strike a deal with the devil and fly through the sky in their canoes. The hunting of Arthur was a much older Frankish/Gallic myth of the spirit of Arthur chasing spirits in the sky. It usually portended bad things to come. It is a curious anomaly to find such a reference in the Journal of the scientific, studious and otherwise dogmatic Galinée but there it stands and its inclusion as a mystical event was meant to be read by Talon in Québec and others in France. Or perhaps it was included as a literary device to alert the reader that temporarily at least, providence had abandoned them and misfortune was coming.

Awakening the next morning, (March 31st approximately) they began construction of their raft. Working all day, they constructed a crude raft made from logs lashed together. Losing the day to constructing the raft meant a further delay before being positioned to reconnect with their canoe borne colleagues and reducing thereby the likelihood of an early rendezvous with them.

Galinée described that day as their most miserable of the entire voyage. Sleeping at night under their blankets on the banks of the river must have tested their stamina and made at least some of the men long for the comparative comforts of the over wintering cabin that they had so recently left. Preparing the raft even as a foot of snow fell, they toiled in the cold, but finally achieved a crossing on their craft, half in and half out of the raft in water with mud and slush up to their waists. Yet none of the men died of hypothermia or exhaustion. They got across and pushed on and found the shoreline where the west edge of Long Point meets Lake Erie. There they saw that the lake on that side of the Point was still filled with floating ice. And so they paused.

They located a ridge of sand where Long Pont joined the mainland and took position there hoping to link up with the four men in the two canoes, if the latter had survived and if they had not given up on the others and had passed by. For them it was their time of hunger. Their provisions were fully exhausted. Dollier and Galinée had gone on reduced rations so the men would have enough strength to go on the hunt. They succeeded in shooting a stag but only a very lean one, the poor creature itself emerging from the starving time of winter. They continued to wait and watch. The night must have seemed one of the longest they had experienced. Yet the next day providential good fortune once again came their way, as on the horizon, the two canoes appeared.   It was nearly Easter and they would celebrate the Resurrection of Christ and their own survival.

The reader might question why the party set out from the wintering site in the midst of what had to be obviously poor conditions? Although the deep winter weather was over it was far from spring-like with the shoreline of Lake Erie still significantly iced as the main ice pack on the lake broke up and was blown ashore and when the woods were nearly impenetrable with un-melted snow deposits.

It may be that it was not a lack of wintering experience that led to the decision to depart Port Dover when they did but that it was a demonstration of learning from their past experiences. They had to leave early to get where they wanted to be, as soon as possible. They had to reach the land of the Potawatomis as quickly as they could so Dollier and perhaps a few of the men could overwinter yet again with whatever Natives might accept them, while the rest of the group under Galinée retraced their steps, or in any event returned to Montréal. It was Galinée's stated intention that he and some of the others would return to Montréal and then travel back again to Dollier as soon as possible. Galinée wrote that they left when they did…

"…so as to get to the Potawatomis at an early date, and that I might be able to return _this year_ (authors emphasis)
to Montréal, in order to send back to M. Dollier the things he would require in his mission."

It was evident that the group would need as much time as possible to reach Montréal before another winter set in stranding them short of their goal. Their initial late departure from Montréal in July had inevitably led to the first overwintering. It would not be to the advantage of Galinée's party to spend another winter in the wilderness before returning to Montréal. The late start of 1669 from Montréal would not be repeated in 1670. **5**

They were men of God and they were physically exhausted. They paused and rested. Their physical condition in late March 1670 could not have been as good as it had been late in the previous year when their first four months of paddling ended. They resolved to remain at Long Point to celebrate Mass and Easter. It also allowed some time for the ice to go out.

On April 8th, two days after Easter, the party set out again, still with four men paddling in the two heavily laden canoes and the other five men pacing them on land. Galinée wrote…

"On Tuesday after Easter, we set out after hearing Holy Mass, and notwithstanding the ice which still lined the entire lake, we launched our canoes and proceeded, still five by land, for two days, to the place of the canoe. As the cold was still very severe, the game was still in the depth of the woods and did not come towards the shore of the great lake. Thus we were short of meat, and were five or six days eating nothing but a little Indian corn cooked in water…"

Their destination was the spot Jolliet had described to them as the location of his "hidden" canoe. The cold was severe. Game remained deep in the woods and there was no hunting. Hunger set in and the prospect of actual starvation loomed. Past the town and hamlets known today as Port Burwell and Port Bruce, they continued with only some small amount of Indian corn (*blé d'Inde* or Sagamite) boiled in water to sustain them. After two days, they arrived at the place where the canoe had been located by the two men Dollier had sent out the previous autumn.

Except that the canoe had vanished.

Jolliet had taken great care to hide his canoe and reveal its precise location to Galinée. Jolliet's description must have been accurate because the two men sent by Dollier to locate it in the Autumn of 1669 reported they had found it, but the canoe had clearly been "discovered" by some person or persons who had in turn hidden it themselves. Galinée believed it was the Iroquois.

For the moment they were in great trouble. They had no guide. They had only two canoes and faced the prospect of continuing in the same fashion as they had since leaving the Wintering Site, which would pose almost insurmountable problems. They had no provisions and their hunting had failed as the men sent out to make a kill did not spot a single animal. They contemplated the idea of making a canoe but the available and necessary wood was not in sap and would not be so for at least another month. Were they to wait for the sap to run and then to build another canoe they would starve. An overland return to Montréal was unthinkable. Not for the first or last time, Galinée said they put the matter in God's hands and prepared for great misery and suffering.

Their luck seemed to have run out (again) when one of the men who was looking for firewood discovered the "Jolliet canoe." **6** It had been moved by an unknown person or persons to the opposite side of the river and well concealed. Providence had saved them once more. Dollier would attribute it to the Grace of God. With three canoes they immediately set out and after one days travel found a large herd of deer which were too far away to track or hunt so that they had to content themselves with shooting an emaciated wolf which was skinned and readied to be put into the kettle. To the French this must have been reminiscent of the offering of dog at Ganondagan. Good luck arrived again at that moment when a small herd of does was spotted. With the entire party acting in concert, they scared the creatures into the water and used their canoes to overtake them, shooting ten of them from their vessels. Taking time to clean and cook the meat and smoke a quantity for future use, they were positioned to carry on to the west, which they did, arriving in due course but very fatigued at Point Pelée.

At Point Pelée, disaster would strike.

HENRI'S STORY
Le Temps de misère

We left the place of our wintering. After that it was terrible. I have never felt such cold and damp. Our provisions were almost gone but we worked hard tramping through the snow and small river valleys. It was as fatiguing as if we had been paddling against the strongest current. Our muscles were not used to such work as we had spent the last two months of our wintering close to our fortified cabin because of the Indians who came by. Besides, we had smoked so much meat in the time leading up to the New Year that there was little need to hunt and the game became sparse and stayed deep in the woods. But all of that changed after we lost one of our canoes and placed our hopes of finding the one hidden by the man named Jolliet. I was one of those who went by land with the Fathers. We met our comrades in the remaining two canoes and I felt there was a chance we would survive.

One night I asked Père Dollier why the land had been claimed for our King as abandoned when there seemed to be a great many Indians here before us. And why we did not claim the lands at the Seneca Village or at Tinaoutoua? He did not get angry. He never got angry. He smiled and told me that it was part of our mission and duty to the King…and that I should not ask any more such questions. So I did not.

CHAPTER 12

Disaster at Point Pelée

Point Pelée

41.35° North Latitude

83.05° West Longitude

1136 kilometers from Island of Montréal

240 kilometers from Wintering Site

*"In this Country one should not start paddling unless one intends
to continue to do so."*

JEAN BRÉBEUF. JESUIT MARTYR. 1649

REFRESHED TO A DEGREE BY their successful hunt of deer, they pressed on in their three canoes with full stomachs and a supply of smoked deer meat. Perhaps it had been all too much.

Galinée wrote that they paddled to a long point shown on his map and landed on the east beach. The only point, other than Long Point, that he shows on his map is a point of land that roughly corresponds to Point Pelée by virtue of its location near the Detroit River and a representation of Island(s) off shore…likely Pelée Island. Both the Point and the Islands would have appeared quite different (as with Long Point) three and a half centuries ago.

Their fatigue was likely cumulative from the wearying trek though the ravines of Norfolk, and the distance they had travelled. Galinée noted that the day of their arrival at Pelée they…*"had made that day nearly twenty leagues so were all very tired."* Assuming that with dead reckoning he was correct and also assuming he used the Maritime League, (see Chapter 14 regarding Galinée's map and his use of Leagues) with 2.5 miles to the League this would mean they paddled on the open lake for 50 miles that day without stopping or resting. Further assuming that by this date it was approximately April 15th, there are 13.5 hours of daylight at that latitude, they would have paddled at almost 4 miles an hour (6.4 km an hour) which is a very fatiguing pace in a twenty foot canoe loaded with men and provisions and making no allowance for wind and waves.

Their fatigue led once again to a mistake and a momentous one at that.

Being too tired to carry their packs up to the high ground they left them on the sand while safeguarding the canoes so as to avoid a repetition of the loss of the canoe like they had experienced near Turkey Point. Of the packs, one in particular contained something as valuable to the success and purpose of their mission as the canoes themselves. Due to their state of exhaustion, specifically stressed by Galinée, and perhaps as an apologia to those reading his account, they went to sleep leaving their packs on the beach. And then a wind arose.

Galinée wrote,

"… a great north east wind rising had time to agitate the lake with so much violence that the water rose six feet where we were and carried away the packs of M. Dollier's canoe, and would have carried away all the rest of us if one of us had not awoke."

Galinée had made several observation of Lake Erie even before the over-wintering. He noted that the waves on Erie rose comparatively to a great height, a factor which he erroneously attributed to its *"great depth."* In fact the very high wave heights on Lake Erie are attributable to the Lakes great length, it's orientation to prevailing winds and its relative shallowness which create large waves that can be very close from wave crest to wave crest.

Having already experienced strong winds at or near Turkey Point, resulting in the loss of his canoe, the phenomenon of water rising so quickly and to such a height was in all probability a "seiche". A seiche is a rapid rise in lake levels caused by strong winds or differential barometric pressure. (see Grady bibliography pp 225-227) The lake's water can be blown against a windward shore and then slop back on the opposite shore as it would as though it was water in giant bath tub. The source (Grady) refers to seiche rising as high as 8.4 feet and in one instance in the Twentieth Century as high as 10 feet. Of all the lakes, Erie experiences the phenomenon the most often. With the sudden onset of the rapidly rising waters and with their packs exposed to the waves there was precious little time to react. Awakened by the roar of the wind Dollier hurried to the beach as his packs had been left closest to the water. Dollier gave the cry *"All is lost!"*

The winds threatened to take all of their baggage but it was the contents of Dollier's canoe that had vanished into the dark waters. Recovery from shore was attempted by lighting pieces of bark but all that was retrieved was a cask of gunpowder and a short time later a musket. Although convenient to recover, none of these items really mattered.

Of greatest significance was that the entire Altar service necessary to perform Mass had gone to the bottom of the lake!

These were no mere "things" or "articles" rather they were the instruments at the core of the Eucharist celebration and were central to their mission. **1** Their plans were shattered. Mass could not be performed amongst themselves or with the Natives. As well, all of their food and provisions were gone save only for what remained in Galinée's canoe. If this was the moment the "Hunting of Arthur" experience had portended, it could not have resulted in a more complete check to Dollier's plans.

Decisions had to be made. The group once again held collaborative discussions. As Galinée wrote they *"deliberated"* amongst themselves and debated options such as finding some other tribe to work with or potentially returning to Montréal to re-provision and obtain another Altar service before returning. This second option was agreed upon. They would return to Montréal, but by what route?

The French certainly knew one route home which was to reverse course and retrace their steps. This would of course necessitate travelling up the Grand River against the current. They could not know if they would necessarily have the same help from the Natives at Tinaoutoua or elsewhere in making the portage to Lake Ontario. They could expect that many of the native men there would be on the hunt. Should they arrive at Lake Ontario they would have to then choose between the north or south shore passage following the shoreline of Lake Ontario to the mouth of the

St. Lawrence. The south shore route would mean passing again through the territory of the Seneca at Ganondagan, mindful of the experiences they had there the first time.

Somewhat surprisingly they did not opt for a passage on the north shore of Lake Ontario even though they knew that some of their compatriots were at Kenté, but neither would they take the south shore route back to Montréal.

As they had travelled west and as Galinée prepared his map, by taking readings of latitude they knew that they had been travelling not only west but also south. The "orientation" of southern Ontario, as pointed out in Chapter One became a determining factor. The Journal relates that Galinée had been taking precise measurements of Latitude with his Jacob's Staff before the arrival at the Wintering Site, but not thereafter. Was it a factor that it had been lost with the canoe contents at Turkey Point or at Point Pelée? In any event they would have appreciated that they were significantly south of Montréal and that by proceeding north they would find themselves on the same latitude as Montréal. Dollier also had his verbal description of the waterways Jolliet had travelled and the map Galinée had made based on the latter"s descriptions.

The decision was made…a decision that might surprise the modern reader. They would return to Montréal via Sault Ste. Marie.

There were Jesuits at the Sault and their Mission was placed among Alkonkian speaking tribes. This would end the interpreter issue since both Dollier and Galinée spoke their language. They were also aware and would be proven correct that large numbers of Natives used the Sault as an assembly point to travel the traditional Nipissing- Ottawa River route back to Montréal. By venturing on this route they would in the end result demonstrate the inter-connectedness of the Lakes, although once again, almost as an apology to their Superiors, Galinée added that they thought they would be more pleased to see a new country than to turn back.

As noted earlier, ever since the days of Champlain all of New France knew of the Nipissing- Ottawa route. It would have been a route that Dollier partly knew of from his over wintering with the Nipissing in 1668-1669. But first they had to get there. Paddling from Pelée to the mouth of the Detroit River they came upon a site that was held by the Iroquois as a spiritual site. At that spot was a large stone idol. The stone *"was all painted, and a sort of face had been formed for it with vermillion."*

Galinée noted that the site had been *"strongly"* commended to them by the Iroquois which must have been either the Iroquois at Tinaoutoua or those who had visited their encampment at Port Dover during the over wintering. It was described to the French as a site where the Iroquois would give thanks when they had safely crossed Lake Erie or when they were about to cross it and where they would leave skins or provisions as gifts of thanks or assurance of a safe passage. That is how Galinée described it in his journal.

However in the commentaries on his map, Galinée described the stone as having two figures of a human on it and that it was where the Iroquois made sacrifices when they were about to go to war.

Perceiving the evidence of native encampments, but no actual Native presence, the French felt that this stone idol had been in some measure responsible for the loss of their Chapel and shortage of provisions. As amongst the French Galinée wrote. *"There was nobody whose hatred it had not incurred."* The French destroyed it. Galinée dedicated one of his few remaining axes to the task at hand and he smashed the stone after which they yoked their canoes together, moved into the water and threw the largest pieces into the river so as to preclude recovery

This curious incident is only explicable through the eyes of the Sulpicians. The action was not only the destruction of an idol but an affirmation to the Natives and more importantly to the Sulpician Superiors in Québec and France that there would be no accommodation of Native beliefs when they came into conflict with those of the Church. Even in 1670, the power of the Church and the secular government in France was becoming more critical of the Jesuits for their increasing "elasticity" in accommodating or incorporating Native practices and some beliefs if they could be brought into Christian fold. The countervailing approach, which the Sulpicians took, was that the dogma and the practices of the Church were not open to variation, even for a noble cause. Such variations indeed could lead to a form of Protestantism and that was not to be allowed.

Dollier and Galinée's act was religiously inspired and politically driven. Reporting the destruction of the idol to their Superiors was in their interest and any Native objections were irrelevant. From the vantage point of the Twenty First Century, it was not their finest hour and would be condemned in any modern context. However the judgement of those in our Century must not engage in "presentism" as author Charles C. Mann defines it (see bibliography *1493* p. 93) "…the projection of contemporary beliefs onto the past."

As other historians have noted, that it was an age when religious tolerance was not a virtue, but a weakness. The Sulpicians were not about to show weakness. After this act of destruction, Galinée observed that they received the providential hand of God as a response to their assault on the idol when they were once more successful in the hunt and provisioned with food again.

Dollier and his men moved on, and so shall we.

Paddling north, and ascending the Detroit River, (against the current) they passed the site of that future American metropolis and Windsor Ontario. The French settlement at Detroit (*Détroit*: French for the Channel, or the Straits) would be founded as a settlement in 1701 by Antoine Laumet de La Mothe, Sieur de Cadillac (1658 -1730). The modern reader might imagine the scene today of the two cities mentioned, with the Ambassador Bridge spanning the river, as freighters and barges pass up and down with the commerce of two Nations, contrasted with the scene in our narrative of nine men in three fragile canoes, paddling hard near the shore, past silent forests and occasional meadows, and no doubt watched by many Native eyes as they travelled.

Paddling against the current and the spring run-off, they would have regained whatever muscle tone had been lost over the winter months and would develop the strength it would take to paddle up that powerful body of water. Steadily they went until they entered Lake St. Clair, (the lake was given its name in later years by La Salle for the Feast of Ste. Claire) a lake which Galinée knew of from his earlier study of the Sanson map (see Figure 6) and from Jolliet's descriptions.

They traversed Lake St. Clair which they called "*the Salt Water Lake*." It is today a distance of approximately 40 kilometers which Galinée estimated as ten Leagues. Then they ascended the St. Clair River, a river that is even longer than the Detroit River.

Figure 20 Satellite Google Image. Point Pélee,, Detroit River, Lake St. Clair, St. Clair River. The Detroit River is 28 miles/44KM long and the St.Clair River is 40.5 miles/65.2KM long. Galinée estimated the St. Clair to be 10 or 12 Leagues in length.

Entering Lake Huron (which Galinée stated also went by the Algonkian term "Michigan") they continued up the lake's eastern coast, going hungry from time to time as the game was not prolific.

Galinée gives some insight into their mindset stating …

" I did not see that anyone became discouraged or troubled…we were accustomed to seeing God aiding us mightily on these occasions that we awaited with tranquility the effects of his bounty, in the thought that He who nourished so many barbarians in these woods would not abandoned His servants."

Weather delayed them from time to time on the exposed eastern shore of Lake Huron but only for a few hours, as opposed to the days of delay they had experienced earlier on Lake Erie while waiting for the lake to calm.

As they approached the tip of the Bruce Peninsula, they had (once again) the good fortune to fall in with three canoes of Natives who were on route to the *Sault* (French for "Rapids"). Thus they acquired guides to take them to the Jesuits. Even during these long days of incessant paddling, Galinée took the time to observe, record and map. Crossing the open lake from modern Tobermory at the tip of the Bruce Peninsula and then to Manitoulin Island, they traversed the south side of Manitoulin and arrived at last on May 25th, at the Jesuit mission at the Sainte-Marie of the Sault.

As they approached the Jesuit mission, whose construction they described as a small Fort, they were advised by the accompanying Natives of the custom of saluting the Fort with several musket shots. This custom would have the effect of completely eliminating the perception of a surprise attack by those in the canoes upon those on shore and it would minimize the possibility from the vantage of those on shore that the approaching force however small, had hostile intent.

*"We were received with all possible charity "*wrote Galinée. They were able to receive the Eucharist as over the preceding month and a half they had been unable to celebrate Mass given the loss of their Chapel service. Since their departure from the Wintering Site and by the time of their arrival at the Sault they had canoed over one thousand kilometers or roughly the same distance as the entire first portion of their journey the year before. No doubt they hoped for rest and respite before leaving for Montréal. There would in fact, be precious little of either.

They were destined leave for Montréal in three days time.

HENRI'S STORY
Vers le Sault

Since we left our winter cabin we covered great distances very quickly. I made my confession to Père Dollier and told him about my doubts. I told him that I wondered if the loss of the sacred Chapel set was not deliberate and that some of the men whose voices had not been heard had set out to lose the Altar set by deliberately leaving his pack on the beach and thus change our sacred mission and avoiding another winter in the forests. We had learned the lesson of safely securing canoes after losing Père Galinée's canoe two days after leaving the wintering site. It struck me as strange. Père Dollier told me to put it out of my mind as such an act would be a great sin.

I asked him if we had been right to destroy the Indian's idol which was important to the Indians as our Eucharist set was to us. Père Dollier told me to have faith that it was but an idol and to place no trust idols or those who venerated spirits of the lakes or the woods.

We paddled the hardest up a narrow but southward flowing great river, un vrai détroit, that flowed into the lake called Erié. Even hugging the shoreline of this river took all our strength and after our rest in the winter we were not in the same condition we had been a few months before. The winter run off of snow made the current féroce. We encountered on another great inland sea and finally we finally arrived at the Mission of the Jesuit Fathers at a place with a great Sault. I thought they could have been more hospitable to us but the Fathers offered us a speedy return to Montréal, with guides, a known route and a journey that promised to be with the current part of the way. I rejoiced. I did not know then of the many portages we would have to make. There was still much to learn.

CHAPTER 13
Sault Ste. Marie and Return to Montréal

Sunday May 25th, 1670

Sault Ste. Marie Jesuit Mission

46.50° North Latitude

84.35° West Longitude

1912 kilometers from Montréal

324 days since departure from Montréal

60 days since departing from Wintering Site

1016 kilometers from Wintering Site

"We were looked upon rather as persons risen from the dead than as common men."

JOURNAL OF GALINÉE

NOTWITHSTANDING HIS KIND SENTIMENTS AT being received by the Jesuits with *"all charity,"* Galinée proceeded to write at length in his Journal in a fashion that was at the very least not laudatory and objectively was somewhat critical of the work performed by the Jesuits at this location.

Noting that Mass was celebrated regularly, he observed that it was exclusively for the twenty to twenty-five Frenchmen habitually present there and that even though the Jesuits had baptized some Natives there were virtually none with enough knowledge or goodwill towards the Church so as to permit them to attend Holy Mass. It struck Galinée as inappropriate to baptize the adults, who manifested little good will towards Christianity and who regarded the Mass as a form of witchcraft. Acknowledging that baptism for those in danger of death might be acceptable, perhaps harkening back to the cannibalized individual he dealt with at the Seneca village, he could find no person except one dying woman who had previously received some Christian instruction and who begged an obliging Dollier to hear her confession.

These criticisms were not meant for public consumption. They were meant for the information of their religious and secular Superiors in Québec and France and were meant perhaps to contrast the substance and style of the Jesuits with the demonstrated zeal of the Sulpicians.

Upon their arrival, Dollier learned that a group of no fewer than thirty canoes of Ottawas had set out for Montréal heading to the Nipissing- Ottawa River route and that another group of *"Kilistinons"* (likely Cree) were to leave shortly. Estimating the distance to Montréal from the Sault of some three hundred leagues they made known to their Jesuit hosts their desire to leave as soon as possible with the declared intention of setting out again from Montréal in the spring of 1671 to try again for the Ohio country.

Their hosts at the Sault were two Jesuit Priests, Fathers Jacques Marquette (1637-1675) and Claude Dablon (1619-1697). First visited by the peripatetic Etienne Brulé in 1610 and named by early French traders as *Sault du Gaston*, the site was frequented for many years by the French but it was only in 1668 that the Jesuit Father Jacques Marquette arrived to establish a permanent mission and named the Rapids in honour of the Virgin Mary. Champlain would mark and name the Sault in his 1632 map although he never traveled there. Dablon would eventually return to Québec and contribute to several parts of the Jesuit Relations. In 1672 Marquette would accompany Louis Jolliet on his journey and thus became the European co-discoverer of the Mississippi.

Dollier also found a Native guide at the Sault and had to pledge payment to him on credit pending their arrival in Montréal. They resolved to follow and catch up with the large group that had previously set out. They departed the Sault three days after their arrival on May 28th, facing a well-known but a very difficult route. They would arrive in Montréal in three weeks time. The final part of their journey would be *more difficult and tiresome than* (one) *could imagine.*

And so they set out once again. Not lacking for food and making particular note of the agreeable abundance of white fish available to them they would need all of the calories they could get for the paddling and the series of portages the like of which none of them would have yet encountered.

This time they followed the northern passage between Manitoulin Island and the mainland until they arrived at the French River. The passage they were about to take to Montréal would be described in great detail over one hundred years later by a giant of Canadian history, the explorer Alexander Mackenzie. In his Journal written over one hundred years later, Mackenzie would describe the Ottawa-Nipissing-French River route as *one of the most dangerous in Canada…where many men have been crushed by canoes.*

Figure 21 Supplies at the Sault.

Numerous portages were encountered with all of the backbreaking and fatiguing labour that they entailed. The reader might note that our travellers would have had longer portages (to and from Tinaoutoua) and a mighty trek around Turkey Point, but none that so frequently involved loading and unloading the canoes as this northern route. When the current favoured the paddler the rapids could sometimes be shot without a portage (an exciting prospect but dangerous too) while at other times, the current, rocks and rough water would guarantee a canoe destroyed and paddlers drowned if a portage was not executed.

The journey on the inside passage of the open lake from the Sault to the western entrance of the French river is trip of approximately two hundred and eighty kilometers and was their first challenge. If the leagues they travelled from Long Point to Pelée had fatigued them earlier then this part of the voyage would require Herculean effort.

There is no mention in the Journal of Dollier and his men actually catching up to the large assemblage of native canoes that had left the Sault two days before but it is likely that they did so. This is probable given that the first group of Natives would have been laden down with their furs for trading at Montréal while our travellers had only their provisions to unload and reload while portaging.

Ascending the French River against the current was almost another one hundred kilometers with a further fifty kilometers trip required to cross the Lake of the Nipissing. Then as now, there is an overland portage to access the Mattawa River which would require a complete emptying of the canoes for the longer portages or their partial emptying at the very least for the shorter ones. The reader should imagine that, in addition to their fatigue from paddling all day long, they were mercilessly persecuted by the hordes of blackflies and mosquitoes that swarm like a biblical plague during those months. Unknown to them Mosquitos can carry disease. One simply had to keep paddling. Finally, travelling eastward with the current on the Mattawa River, they faced a further trip of over five hundred kilometers to Montréal down the Ottawa River, a voyage that was an inevitable death trap for those unaware of the rapids, whirlpools and rocks.

Galinée remarked on the ever present prospect of death by being swallowed up *"in places that looked frightening"* (*effroyables*).

Figure 22 French River Rapids by Paul Kane 1845

The skill of the man steering the canoe the *"avant"* at the front of each canoe, was critical with little margin for error. Sometimes there was as little as a coins width of space available between the rocks and the skin of the canoe, while skimming past rocks in the rivers as the spring snow melt fed the volume of water. Galinée gives some insight into the skill of the seven soldiers, noting that they had knowledge of the challenges and were not *"novices"* in those specific channels. He even gave a rare nod to the skill of their Native guide, a person he described as *"very good."*

Because of the spring run-off, Galinée wrote that had they been travelling in the other direction, that is to say towards the Sault, they would have encountered at least forty-five or fifty portages but as it was, traveling with the current, with high water levels, with the expertise of the men and the guide, they *"saved"* seventeen or eighteen such portages in their overall descent of the Ottawa River.

However motivated they were, and whatever reserves of zeal remained in their souls, their physical limits had been reached. In eighty-four days since their departure from the Wintering Site, including the final twenty-two days of *"the most fatiguing travel he* (Galinée) *had done in his life,"* they had paddled almost two thousand kilometers!

It was the year 1670.

In France, King Louis XIV had entered into the secret Treaty of Dover with the bankrupt King Charles II of England and agreed to pay him a large annual secret subsidy on conditions which if publicly known, would likely have led Charles to the scaffold and the same fate as his late father. In May of that year, Charles II would create the Hudson's Bay Company by Royal Charter. The French playwright Molière presented his play *"Le Bourgeois Gentilhomme"* at Court. In England, a young Isaac Newton continued his study on optics and the refraction of light. In Carolina, one hundred and fifty settlers arrived to found the future colony of Charleston. England returned Acadia to France after an occupation of over a decade. **1** In the Spring of that year 1670 as these world events unfolded, nine exhausted men in three canoes made the final descent of the Ottawa River and no doubt dreamt of the world they had left behind and would soon re-enter.

The Ottawa River flowing towards the St. Lawrence widens to form the Lake of Two Mountains. Traversing the lake into Lac St. Louis at its southern extremity Dollier and his eight companions finally turned east. There must have been a moment when someone on shore or a lookout on the palisaded garrison walls at Montréal saw a small group of canoes approaching the shore. A call would have gone out and then slowly recognition dawned to those onshore as to the identity of those in the canoes. It was almost a year since they had departed the settlement of Montréal. And Galinée had contracted malaria.

He had fallen ill near the end of the trip with what he described as tertian fever *(une fièvre tierce)*. **2** Dollier and his companions had arrived in Montréal. It was June 18th, 1670.

Abbé de Queylus and the other Montréalais greeted them as though *"they were persons risen from the dead."* One might wonder what specifically had reached the ears of the Montréalais, from La Salle, or a member of his party, since La Salle had predicted certain death for the Sulpicians at Tinoutoua. In fact Galinée attributed this premature news of their death to La Salle and his party, writing in the Journal upon his return to Montréal that *"the latter…indeed announced as soon as they arrived here,* (following their departure from Tinaoutoua) *and caused a great deal of pain to those who took an interest in our persons."*

When the last paddle stroke had been taken, no doubt days and nights followed with all nine of the men telling others of their adventure. But there was still work to be done. And Galinée, however ill he was had a Journal to write and a map to draw. The Map had to be accurate. It was important. It was going into the hands of the Intendant Jean Talon and then it was going to be sent to Louis XIV, King of France who would learn of the names of Dollier and Galinée and also learn of the voyage that they had made on his behalf.

It would be the legacy of their voyage.

HENRI'S STORY
Chez-nous

We were going home! We left the Holy Jesuit Fathers and started back to Montréal. These days were the hardest paddling we had yet encountered as the Indians we paddled with were not as fatigued as we were and were possessed of their own zeal to arrive first in Montréal with their furs for trade so they could get the best price and so they could begin the journey back to their homes. It seemed we were always paddling against the current and that the portages were more frequent than anything we had met until then. We kept up with the Indians.

Finally, at the lake called Nipissing, where Father Dollier had travelled only the year before, did we gain the advantage of the current and upon reaching the River of the Ottawas, the current became very strong in our favour but with many portages. If we did not have the knowledge of the Indians and Père Dollier, who told us when to get out of our canoes we would surely have perished. At last I recognized the waters of the Great River of Canada where we had started and when we landed at Montréal, the inhabitants looked upon us with amazement.

I returned to the garrison as a soldier and remained as a soldier for a few years until I obtained the grant of a small farm plot on the Island of Montréal. I wanted no more of paddling into the wilderness and only did so once the year after our return when the Governor Courcelle sent a large body of men to the mission at Kenté on the Lake of the Iroquois.

That was the last time I saw the great inland sea. I told my comrades what we had seen and done. Not all of them believed me. But the Holy Fathers wrote about all these events for I saw both of them writing things during our voyage. And now I have told my blessèd sister what I saw all those years ago so she may record what I remembered.

CHAPTER 14

Revelations, the Journal & the Map

Wednesday June 18th, 1670

Island of Montréal

348 Days since departure from Montréal

2900 Kilometers travelled since departing Montréal

74 Days since departing Wintering site

2003 Kilometers travelled since departing Wintering site

987 Kilometers from Sault Ste. Marie

21 Days from Sault Ste. Marie

GALINÉE'S MAP ARRIVED IN FRANCE along with his Journal and the Procès Verbal. They were viewed as important and were shown to the King, Louis XIV. As part of his original instructions, and consistent with his specific skill set, for which he had been chosen to make the trip, Galinée created his annotated map. The map itself was a remarkable achievement.

Before his departure, Galinée was tasked by de Queylus to create a trustworthy map and one with sufficient detail to *"enable me to find my way back again from any place...in the woods and rivers of* (the) *country."* With his usual Sulpician modesty, Galinée described his skill at mathematics as a mere "smattering" (*une teinture des mathématiques*). Yet when taking his latitude on the south shore of Lake Erie he would identify the sun's north "declination" and its "equinoctial distance from the zenith, "all suggesting that he was possessed of a reasonably deep mathematical ability, which he applied to his map making.

At first view the map itself is a curious one to the modern eye, until inverted. North is not at the top of the map but at the bottom. For a modern reader to make sense of the map with features familiar to the eye, it is necessary to turn the map upside down making contemporaneous reading of Galinée's annotations impossible.

Why then might North be depicted at the bottom of the map? A possible answer is that when using a Jacob's staff in the northern hemisphere as Galinée did, it is necessary to "shoot the sun" or measure the angle between the sun and the horizon in order to determine degrees of latitude.

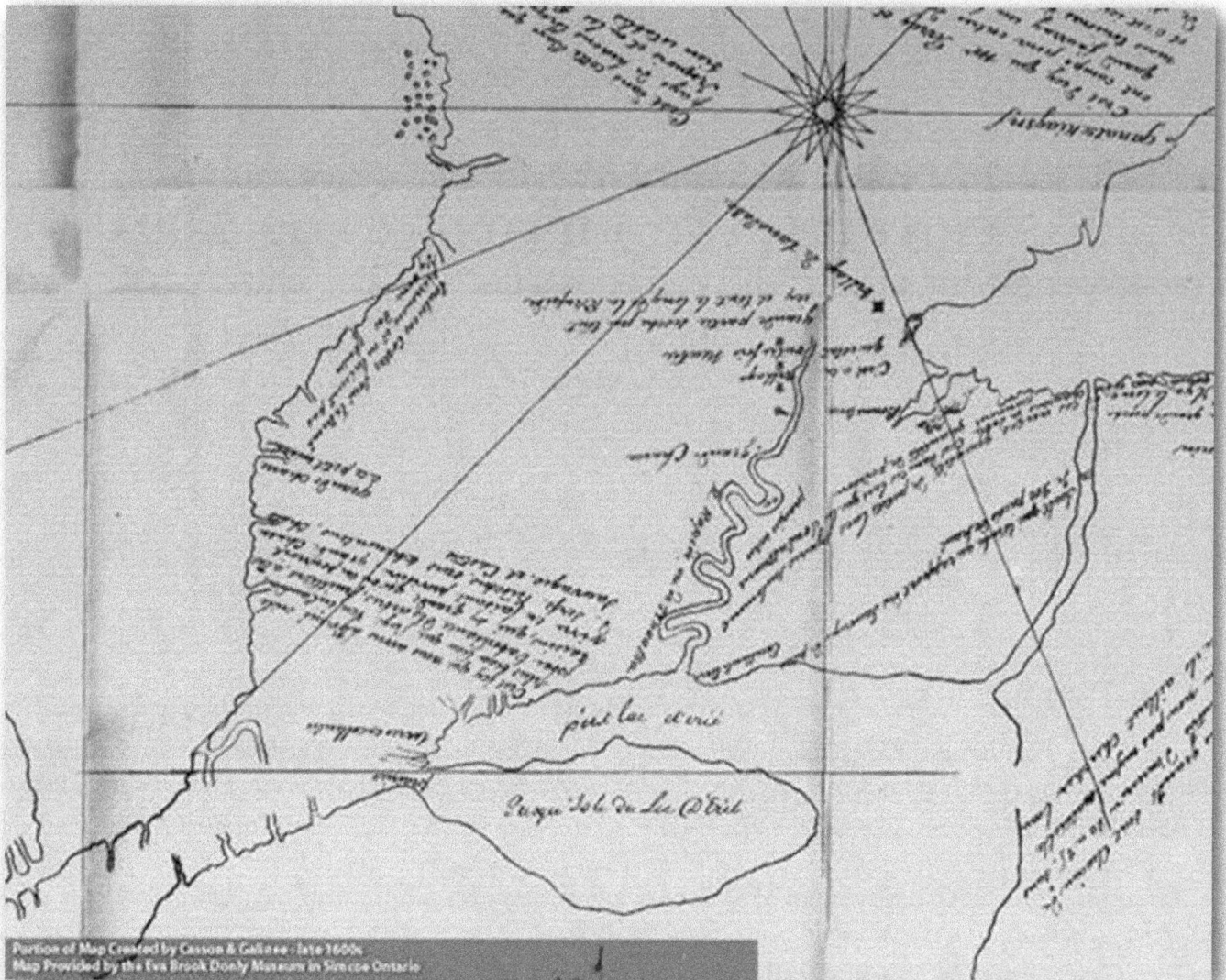

Figure 23. Part of Galinée's map of 1670 (Courtesy Norfolk Historical Society) shown inverted in this image with north at the top of the image and hence most of the comments appear upside down. The mouth of the Grand River and the place of the over wintering at Port Dover are depicted. Two annotations are readable in this configuration being *pétit lac d'érié* for the Inner Bay and *Presqu'Isle du Lac D'Erie* for Long Point. All other annotations appear upside down until the map is inverted as Galinée drew it, with south at the top of the map.

Without modern clocks, noon is the one time each day, cloud cover permitting, that allows an accurate telling of time. In the northern hemisphere the sun at noon is in the southern half of the sky. The navigational "anchor" therefore lies to the south. The navigation of Galinée was not by magnetic compass or the north star as might be used by ships at sea but by the one certainty of the cosmos, that at noon the sun is at its highest in the sky and from that one's latitude can be determined. Even until the 19th Century aboard ship in England's Royal Navy, all clocks were checked against the sun at noon.

Latitude told one how far north or south one had travelled. Longitude depended on dead reckoning or a sense of how many hours one had traveled in an east/west direction. Galinée's map was, as he described it, a marine chart and he employed dead reckoning methods (*les rumbs de vent*) as sailors did. Precise longitudinal mapping would not be possible for almost a century after our traveller's journeys until accurate clocks were invented. This explains why the maps north-south configurations are, to a degree, superior to the east-west representations on the map. The map was meant to be a guide for future travellers. With his scientific and mathematical training, Galinée sought to create a tool that would be informative to those who might follow or who might be encouraged to follow upon instructions from France.

The map was to be read along with its many descriptive annotations as well as in conjunction with the Journal which would give accurate impressions of distances by describing calendar dates and numbers of days paddled. Even on the very challenging descent of the Ottawa River, Galinée would not fail to note in detail on the map the number of portages along with some features such as their length or degree of difficulty, much as a modern travel guide might tell the motorist what to find along the highway. In summary, the map would be quite sufficient for anyone to retrace their route even to the exacting standards of the Minister Colbert in France.

In his Journal Galinée would often relate distances in "leagues." As previously noted there were different lengths of leagues in use at the time including a league used for ships. Galinée stated that he reduced Jolliet's description of the location of the hidden canoe to a "marine" chart and that the map was also made as a marine chart as he was *"more familiar with these (marine) maps than with the geographical ones and moreover the former are commonly more exact than the others."*

Therefore it is more likely than not that the distances he relates are "nautical" leagues. However the use of leagues in his Journal was not Galinée's strong point, as at times he would describe distances in leagues that in no way correspond to geographical reality then or now. By way of example his description of the leagues they travelled from the Wintering Site westwards exceeds the entire length of the Lake Erie.

The original Galinée map was lost but not before it was carefully copied in the Nineteenth Century by multiple historians. The last known original copy likely went up in flames with other government records during the Commune in Paris in 1870. Before that time, one American and one Frenchman had painstakingly copied the map and as stated in his scholarly work of 1903, James Coyne was satisfied with the exactitude of the copies that have come to us in the modern era.

In 1687, in order to press its claim to territory in North America and just prior to embarking yet again on another war, (the Nine Years War of 1688-1697) France sent a copy of the map and the Procès Verbal to the English to demonstrate their primacy to the lands claimed. No response was received from the English.

The original Journal and Procès Verbal still can be found in the National Library of France. The commentaries on the copied map correspond with the contents of the Journal. Finally, Galinée states that he marked only what he had seen so that except for the north shore of Lake Ontario, which was likely filled in by Trouvé or Fénélon, the larger part of the south shore of Lake Erie is not depicted on the map.

Cleary it was the intent of Talon to see that the most complete overview of the lower lakes should be sent to France. In writing on the map and repeating in the Journal that he had recorded only that which he had seen, Galinée was creating an author's "certification" that he was responsible for those contents he had penned. It was the first map of the lower Lakes drawn by one who had actually been there.

Dollier also took the time to write his own Journal for as he stated in his subsequent work *"History of Montréal,"* (see bibliography) in comparing the two he considered Galinée's to be superior so he destroyed his. As noted in the opening Chapters of this work, this may be sad for history but it serves something as a further guarantee of the accuracy of the contents of Galinée's Journal from a reliable source who had little motive to distort or falsely praise.

In the text of Galinée's Journal and even on the map Galinée employs the practice of the time in referring to Dollier not as *Père Dollier* but as M. Dollier, (*Monsieur Dollier*) which practice was included on the map sent to France wherein our travellers are referred to as *"Mess'rs Dollier et Galinée Missionaires du Seminaire de St Sulpice."*

Arriving in Montréal in June, the Journal was written quickly thereafter by Galinée and clearly drafted with an eye to detail but also on the calendar since what he wrote would have to be delivered to Québec, read there, and then put on board a ship before the last sailing to France in September. The text of the journal is strongly suggestive that Galinée made continuous notes during his journey and compiled the final version from those. Clearly, Talon and others had input to the map as they included some commentary (but not in the Journal) with respect to what could be found on the north shore of Lake Ontario, a region Galinée had never been to and a place that Dollier would himself only visit briefly in 1671 after the map had been sent to France.

Galinée stated that he was not in full health upon arrival in Montréal but still he was able to write the Journal in final form and have Dollier compare his own writings to Galinée's efforts. The task of compiling the Journal and the map took significant effort because even as they arrived at Montréal, Galinée was suffering from the debilitating symptoms of malaria. Sweating, aches, flu-like symptoms and intermittent convulsive shaking would have punctuated Galinée's writing efforts. And he was exhausted. Galinée described his twenty-two day passage from Sault Ste. Marie as the most fatiguing travelling he had ever done. This from a man who had paddled against the current of the St. Lawrence and later the Detroit River and St.Clair Rivers.

Together, the Map, the Journal and Procès Verbal claim of lands were sent to France for Colbert's immediate review, likely by late August or early September. In his History of Montréal, Dollier noted that the ships left for France that year at the end of October and before the St. Lawrence River froze. The significance of the map was sufficiently apparent to Talon that once the "revisions" were done by way of additions (such as the north shore Lake Ontario and related commentaries) he dispatched a second ship to catch up to the vessels that had departed earlier carrying the Journal. That he sent out a corrected version of the map on a vessel in November of that year demonstrates the importance he placed on what Dollier and Galinée had found.

When the Map, Journal and Procès Verbal reached France, Colbert almost immediately issued instructions that a process similar to if not identical to the one carried out at the Wintering Site was to be conducted elsewhere in New France on every possible occasion. With that Directive reaching New France, as related in Chapter 11 it came to pass that in 1671 at Sault Ste. Marie, that a large Cross bearing the Arms of France was raised in the presence of the French and as many Natives as could be assembled. The land was similarly claimed for Louis XIV. The actions at the Wintering Site of Port Dover had set the precedent.

Finally, having read and re-read Galinées Journal many, many times there was a certain aspect that struck this writer. Even in times when Dollier's group were *"misérable"* as when ascending the St. Lawrence, or when they were near starvation after leaving the wintering place, Galinées Journal has a consistent tone of optimism. It is not just a question of what he says but "how" he says it. Like the impression a witness might make in a trial while testifying, sometimes form can be as impressive as content. This may be a function that the final form the journal was created upon the return to Montréal but it paints a picture of a man who never completely despaired. Galinée was confident that they would succeed or at the very least get through with the aid of a providential God.

France had expected much of Dollier and Galinée and in this respect they not only met those expectations but exceeded them.

CHAPTER 15

Dénouement

Saint- Germain-en-Laye

Palace of Louis XIV

48.89° North Latitude

2.097° East Longitude

5,502 Kilometers from Ville Marie and the Island of Montréal

" In the great ocean of time, all men swim together. "

DANIEL BOORSTIN. *THE CREATORS.*

DOLLIER'S CANADIAN TRAVELS WERE NOT quite yet over. In the following year of 1671, Courcelle was troubled by what he saw as increasing hostilities between the Iroquois and the Ottawa. The reader will recall that these troubles had been brewing as early as the time of Jolliet's acquisition of the Iroquois slave at Sault Ste. Marie. With an effective veil of secrecy, Courcelle assembled a force of men and heavy flat bottomed boats which he transported to Cataraqui (Kingston) from Montréal. This signaled a clear intention to the Iroquois that the French could and would move heavy craft and equipment past the Lachine rapids in the event of conflict. Dollier went with him. It was his last sojourn to Lake Ontario and the Pays d'en Haut.

When La Salle left Dollier at Tinaoutoua, the most trustworthy sources put him back on the Ottawa River by the summer of 1670 and then later in Montréal, desperately seeking funds. He would struggle his entire life to secure funds (which he usually did) and to lose the money (nearly always) while seeking discovery and self-aggrandisement. That he seemed able to convince men to follow him and maintain the ear of authority is remarkable. Some later apologists for La Salle suggested that on leaving Dollier's party La Salle discovered the Ohio and the Mississippi (later named by the French the *"Colbert"* River before reverting to its ancient Native name) but if La Salle had done so he would have trumpeted the fact to the world. The Mississippi River would be discovered by the brother of Adrien Jolliet, Louis Jolliet and the Jesuit Jacques Marquette in 1673.

When he left Dollier and Galinée, La Salle had two routes to choose from. He could have followed the North Shore of Lake Ontario, a route that Adrien Jolliet would have been familiar with, at least east of the Rouge River (See Endnotes 1 and 5 for Chapter 8). Yet had he done so he might have encountered the Sulpicians at Kenté. Neither Trouvé nor Fénélon ever made any mention of his passing by.

Or La Salle could have followed the south shore of Lake Ontario essentially retracing his steps back towards Montréal. Not only was this route known to him (and he was paying dearly for his crew) but it would have been most attractive to Jolliet's native companion by putting him near his homeland. This route would also alert the

Seneca that La Salle was returning without Dollier and his men and perhaps, just perhaps was the trigger that caused the Iroquois to go looking for Dollier and "stumble" (if that's what it was) upon the over wintering encampment at Port Dover.

La Salle would later establish and build the first Fort Frontenac at what is now Kingston, Ontario. In 1678-79 he would build a sailing vessel on Lake Erie, the *Griffon* and sail it the following year to the upper lakes only to have the vessel later vanish without a trace, when he ordered it to proceed without him back to Lake Erie. He likely derived some benefit from Galinée's map concerning Long Point and the layout of the Lakes. It was probable that La Salle stopped once more at Ganondagan while on route to build the *Griffon*, this time with the Récollet Priest Louis Hennepin, if the latter's account is considered reliable. He also likely passed by the Port Dover wintering site in the early 1680's by land while returning along the north shore of Lake Erie to Montréal from the Illinois country.

Later, in 1682 La Salle would be the first European to travel the full length of the Mississippi River, demonstrating its connection with the Gulf of Mexico. He would secure the important patronage of Governor Frontenac. Travelling to France in 1683, he would convince the French Court that his successful navigation of the Mississippi's lower reaches (noting he had claimed it for France and named it after his Sovereign...Louisiana) would permit the French to cut off Spanish advancement in the Gulf of Mexico. It was at this time his hubris and deceit would cost him everything. Sailing from France with three vessels he overshot the Mississippi by several hundred miles. The expedition fell apart and he led a group of his men inland and eastward to find the great river. His arrogance finally led to mutiny and on March 19th, 1687 he was murdered by his own men in what is now Texas. 1

La Salle's brother Jean, the Sulpician Priest had accompanied Robert on the Texas mission. He kept his brother's death a secret even when the small remainder of the party got back to Montréal. This permitted Jean to realise on his brothers assets before creditors could seize them. Unlike the Jesuits the Sulpicians were not bound by an oath of poverty. Jean sailed for France, where he wrote a somewhat fanciful book about his brother's exploits and died in 1722 at Rouen, a rich man.

There are towns and parks in both the United States and Canada named after René-Robert Cavelier Sieur de La Salle. His complex life and death still resonnates across the history of two nations.

Jean Talon was without doubt the most talented and driven Intendant New France ever had. He was the most energetic of all Intendants and vigorously promoted industry and colonisation in New France. No subsequent Intendant would surpass him in this. Sadly, his visions for New France were not shared conceptually or financially with Colbert or the Court in France which was engaged in expensive wars in Holland and elsewhere. Although he promoted immigration to New France and did all he could to see that no one of age was left unmarried, thus enabling the population to increase, he himself never married and died in 1694 in France age sixty-eight.

Rémy de Courcelle, the Governor of New France who led the 1666 expedition of the Carignan-Salières Regiment, the expedition that served as a school for the freshly arrived Dollier, returned to France in 1672. According to the *Dictionary of Canadian Biography* one of his last acts in Canada was to leave a sizeable sum in the care of Dollier for the benefit of a six year old Iroquois girl he had adopted and placed in the care of Nuns in Québec. What an interesting bequest this was from a man who had waged a scorched earth policy against the Mohawk.

Courcelle died unmarried in France at age 72.

De Queylus's disagreements with Laval over certain matters had earlier resulted in his being ordered to return to France and then ordered by the King himself not to leave the Country. Disobeying, he travelled back to Canada until he was ordered by Louis to return once again across the ocean. Only in 1668 was he permitted to return as Superior of the Seminary of Ville Marie. It was then that he ordered the Dollier expedition as well as a Sulpician mission to the Kenté (near Port Hope) and others. De Queylus returned to France in 1671 to settle some matters relating to his late father's estate. He never again returned to Canada and died in 1677.

The Seneca found peace with the French but not with their Native neighbors and continued fighting with the Susquehannocks (Andastes) to the south until 1679. They would barely enjoy a decade of peace. A later Governor of New France, Jacques-René de Brisay de Denonville, anticipating an Iroquois alliance with the English opted for a pre-emptive strike. In 1687 he brought a large force of soldiers and Canadians through the lands of the Seneca, and destroyed their Village of Ganondagan and other Seneca villages as well. It was under his command that some of the captured Iroquois were sent to France to serve as galley slaves in the harbour of Marseilles. Thus provoked, in August of 1689 the Seneca attacked the Island of Montréal en masse with over 1000 warriors. There were many casualties on both sides and there would be no peace until 1701.

For his part Denonville contemplated attacking Albany and then New York so as to make them French possessions and give New France thereby an ice free port. He might have succeed had he actually tried and history would have been very different. As it was, he was recalled to France, not because of any shortcomings but because he was seen as an effective military commander in the European War that Louis XIV was about to unleash.

With the American Revolutionary War, (1775-1783) the Six Nations (the Tuscarora having been admitted to the Confederacy) had to choose sides. Many fought with the English and when the colonies were lost to the Americans they were granted land by the Swiss born British General and Governor General Sir Frederick Haldimand along the banks of the Grand River, in which community their descendants live to this day. The Territory of the Haudenosonee, the Six Nations of the Grand, is bisected by the River Dollier and Galinée both briefly knew.

When John Graves Simcoe first arrived in Toronto Harbour in 1793, he encountered only Mississauga's, members of the Ojibwa or the Anishanabee (the "people") as they call themselves. The North Shore Iroquois were gone and Tinaoutoua had long since been abandoned.

The Voyage of Dollier and Galinée was the single greatest effort and the high point of Sulpician exploration in seventeenth century. There would not be another venture like it notwithstanding Dollier's desire to venture out again. Apart from a brief visit in 1670, by Trouvé to Tinaoutoua, made at Dollier's written request, even the Kenté mission would be ultimately abandoned by the Sulpicians. The Sulpicians turned their talents to the creation of the Sulpician Seminary and the administration of the Island of Montréal.

When it comes to pass in 2017 that Montréal celebrates the 375th Anniversary of its founding, leading the list of those whose history has been integral to that of the City will be the Sulpicians in general and Francois Dollier de Casson in particular.

The Jesuit Order to which Frémin and Marquette and the martyred Brébeuf belonged would continue to thrive and expand for a period of time. It would be the Jesuits (and the Récollets) who accompanied French explorers deep into the North American continent. In the early 18th Century, the Jesuits would develop a Canadian commercial venture not in furs but in exporting wild Ginseng to China through their religious houses and agents there.

Seen as a competing power to the autocratic rulers of Europe, the Jesuit Order was abolished by the Pope in 1773, whose directive was ignored in Prussia and elsewhere and with the downfall of Napoleon Bonaparte, the Jesuits revived, found their former sea legs and became once again a world-wide force to be reckoned with.

In the Place Royale in the lower town of Québec, there is a copy of a bust by the sculptor Lorenzo Bernini of Louis XIV, le Roi-Soleil, King of France. The longest reigning French Sovereign would lead his country to artistic and literary glory. He would seek military glory but would discover that the human and financial cost can be ruinous. He was late in the game in focussing attention on empire beyond the hexagon of mainland France and his expenditures on Versailles would cripple his freedom of action.

It was in his name though that French explorers would claim lands that straddled Acadia (which he would lose in 1714) to Hudson Bay, and from Québec to the headwaters of the Mississippi and down its length to the Gulf of Mexico. When he died, the admiration of his countrymen had largely evaporated with over one million French dead as a result of his wars. He advised his grandson *"Do not imitate me in the taste I had for building or for war."* (Durant p. 719) Amidst general rejoicing he died on September 1ˢᵗ, 1715 at age 77.

Galinée did not long remain in Canada, departing for France in the Autumn of 1671 on the same vessel as de Queylus. Upon his return to France, he was ordained as a Priest. He worked at the Saint-Sulpice Parish and Mount Valérian as well. In 1677 after asking permission from the Superior of Saint Sulpice, he relocated to the Séminaire de Saint-Sulpice at Issy-les-Moulineaux.

While on route to Rome, he died on August 16ᵗʰ, 1678 age thirty-three. Accessible records of the Archives of Saint-Sulpice do not reveal the cause of his death or the location of his grave. Perhaps it was the Tertian fever that cut him down in his prime.

Francois Dollier de Casson is the central figure of this story even if Galinée was his spokesman. After his brief excursion to Lake Ontario in 1671 his life would center on Montréal and Québec.

His talents as a religious leader and wise administrator would not go untapped. A few years after his journey he would be named the Superior of the Sulpicians at Montréal and hence the civil administrator of the entire Island. He had to deal with disputes and property matters as between the citizenry. His beloved Seminary was his chief interest and time-taker. Dollier seemed possessed of a serenity of character such that if he encountered a detractor or a critic over an issue any hostile sentiment toward him quickly passed given the essential fairness of the man. In time he would be named Vicar-General of Québec, second only to the Bishop of Canada.

Dollier was the first historian of Montréal penning a lengthy history from its founding in 1642 to the date of its writing circa 1673. He was modest and only rarely identified himself in the text when describing such events as his 1666 work at Fort Ste. Anne or on the Voyage with Galinée.

Figure 24 Purportedly Dollier in his later years.

In early 1672, he suffered an injury when he fell through the ice and spent several hours in frigid water before being extricated. His health suffered and remained poor for a considerable time. In 1674 he sailed for France and was gone for four years. He lived with his sister and her family there. His second sister was by that time Superior of a Convent of Benedictine nuns in Angers in the West of France. In 1678, Dollier said goodbye to his family and for the final time, sailed to Canada, coincidentally on the same ship as La Salle who had travelled to France to promote the programs of his benefactor, Governor Frontenac. **2**

Upon his return Dollier was tireless in becoming the modern city's first town planner and completing his design for street improvement in the growing town of Montréal. When the modern visitor walks on Rue Saint Paul or Rue Notre Dame and others in Vieux Montréal, one should recall that these streets were laid out by Dollier.

Dollier was possessed of what would today be called situational awareness. It no doubt developed from his years as a soldier. He knew how to respond quickly to crisis and how to deal with danger. He also applied this awareness to his New World situation as demonstrated by his effective response at Fort Ste. Anne. Finally his social astuteness served him for many years in navigating the political minefields (a modern metaphor to be sure) of New France in the struggles between Intendants and Governors, and between the civil authorities and the strong willed Bishop.

When he became the Superior of the Sulpicians in Montréal he became in effect, the Seigneur of the Island. Dollier granted land on the Island of Montréal to both the Jesuits and the Récollets. To him they were not "competitors "of the Sulpicians.

It was Dollier ahead of his time, who sought to build a canal that we would now call the Lachine canal. Then as today, infra-structure cost overruns caused concern in France and he was reminded by his Superiors in France to focus on the Seminary.

Figure 25 Sulpician Seminary, Montréal

In recent years, some pop-culture books have been written using historic personages as Chief Executive Officer's of large corporations. One can find titles such as "Elizabeth I, CEO "...or "Napoleon as CEO". Dollier was the Chief Executive Officer of the Sulpicians and his key to success, other than his sincere piety, was based on perseverance, belief in the cause at hand and taking care of one's people be they Seminarians or soldiers paddling canoes.

Of the distant river Dollier sought to reach, the beautiful river, the Ohio, one can stand in the shadow of the sports stadiums of modern Pittsburgh, where the Alleghany and Monongahela Rivers meet to form the Ohio, and see the outline of a French fortification built after 1670. This site would have been the initial prime destination of our travellers had the Altar set not been lost.

Should the reader visit Ganondagan Seneca Longhouse in Upstate New York, at the State Park at Broughton Hill or visit the Wintering Site in Port Dover or pass over the Grand River, the Detroit River or the Ottawa River, perhaps they will take a moment to reflect what was it like three hundred and fifty years ago. Hopefully, by this text the reader will have some sense of how it might have looked and how beautiful it must have been.

There is a Lake in Québec named after Dollier and one for Galinée as well. It would no doubt please Galinée greatly to know that there is an elementary school named after him in Northern Québec and an École Sécondaire named after him in Cambridge Ontario, not too far from where the travellers would have portaged from Tinaoutoua to the Grand River.

At the west end of Montreal Island there is a "Dollier de Casson" park that has a lovely bicycle path that follows part of the canal system he sought to build. With what can only be historic irony, the park is located in the Community of LaSalle.

He lived just long enough to witness the signing of peace in 1701 between New France, the Iroquois and the Natives of the Pays d'en Haut after more than ten years of war.

Francois Dollier de Casson, a soldier of old France and an explorer of New France, Priest of Saint-Sulpice, died on September 27th, 1701 at the age of sixty-five and was buried in the Parish Church of Notre Dame in his beloved Montréal.

CHAPTER 16

Conclusion

———

I CONCLUDE THIS HISTORY NOT only with the fictional Henri but with the equally fictional Siouqori (a name whose origin will be clear to the attentive reader) to show the "other "perspective. This narrative was written through the author's his own euro-centric lens based upon an equally euro-centric text written by Galinée. There is another way of looking at things.

Some might posit that the voyage was a failure given that it did not achieve its original objectives of establishing contact with the Potawatomis and proselytizing there. If however the index of success was to record and map their travels so that others might follow, then from the perspective of French national interests it was a resounding success.

Before their journey, no European had travelled and recorded the lower great lakes. No one had travelled from Lake Ontario to Lake Erie and positioned themselves near the portages that would permit travel to the Ohio and the Mississippi. After Dollier, everyone wanting to travel to the middle of America would take the route he had revealed, eventually leading to the construction of a series of French Forts down the Mississippi and its tributaries. Jacques Marquette and Louis Jolliet take credit for discovering the Mississippi for the French. La Salle has credit for descending that river for its entire length. But neither event might have happened when it did, by whom it did, without the preliminary exploration by Dollier and Galinée. They showed the way.

As other historians have noted, in 1666 New France was a small colony made up of three settlements hugging the St. Lawrence. By 1701 it would be comprised of the better part of North America from Acadia and Newfoundland with a huge swath running through the middle of the future United States. This beginning of empire had as part of its own beginning, the journey of Dollier and Galinée.

It might also be said that Dollier's greatest successes lay ahead of him following his return to Montréal. His achievements in municipal governance and construction reveal the man to be a visionary. His talents at mediating disputes between the church and state and within the Order itself were highly valued and respected. It may be that his mission always did lie in calming the souls of his own countrymen versus converting those First Nations who were perfectly happy with their own world view. His fulfillment as a peace maker would be found in his work amongst his own countrymen.

This saga is not just one of Europeans exploring lands unknown to them, but a chronicle of a land completely known and mastered by the native population without whose direction help and guidance the Frenchmen would likely not have succeeded or even likely have survived.

Except for the time of the over wintering in which the French did very well, and the departure from Port Stanley, at all other times Dollier and Galinée had actual help from the Natives, or directions provided by them or as guides. As well there was the invaluable wintering expertise and leadership provided by Dollier and clearly a certain "democratic" aspect to his leadership given the several Councils or consultations he held with his men. This would not be something any of La Salle's men then or in any of that adventurer's future expeditions would experience.

There is one person whose ultimate fate is unknown but for whom this writer, perhaps somewhat fancifully, hopes ended thus. It is likely that the original slave, the man held by the Nipissing Chief Nitarikyk when tasked by Dollier to accompany the Dutchman to go and find Jolliet's canoe, simply slipped away and returned to his people in the south west. His story is an escape story. He listened to Dollier, spoke to de Queylus who wrote the concept letter and when the journey was undertaken and included him it effectively moved this man closer to his freedom every day. One can only imagine his smile as he struck out, free at last from the French on an open if difficult route home.

Good fortune, luck, pure chance or divine providence as Galinée would call it arrived often and kept the expedition going. The fact that Frémins interpreter was at Ganondagan was the first such event followed by the arrival of the Native from Fort Orange who offered to guide them. Encountering Jolliet at Tinaoutoua when a few days difference might have caused them to miss each other was remarkable as was the parties luck that the latter's canoe had not been destroyed or taken and was ultimately found. To draw on the earlier parallel, if a space journey depended on such timely luck it surely would have ended in disaster. There is nothing that is inevitable in history. It was not pre-ordained that they would survive. But they did.

There were then several stories that emerge from Galinée's Journal and it is this lesson that became clear to this writer as I read and re-read the Journal for what it said and what it omitted to say and what it ultimately conveyed to me.

The first story could be described as the simple linear journey. Nine men in three canoes travelled from Montréal around the lower Great Lakes and returning to what was to them "civilization."

The second story was a journey of the mind, a seventeenth century mind, that of Galinée, whose thoughts and motives are revealed to us three and a half centuries after his death. The French view of the Natives and their world is part of that story. Sometimes the French admired the Natives, sometimes they disparaged them or feared them. They almost always sought them out and needed them.

A third story or theme is revealed in the Journal but it is perhaps more subtly told. When the travellers left Montréal on that July day in 1669 they perceived that they were completely leaving civilization except for the small vestiges of home that they could carry into a wilderness otherwise peopled by "savages" or even as they occasionally called them "barbarians." In fact it is clear that they were travelling from one civilization into the midst of another well established and very successful civilization, that of the Natives who had managed quite well, not for a single over wintering season but for tens of thousands of years.

It would be Native civilization, its people, devices, towns, food and knowledge that would see the French safely returned back to their own world. The French only rarely acknowledged this. In this failure to fully acknowledge their contribution we must hearken to the words of a great Canadian historian W.J. Eccles, we must "examine the events by the light and customs of the era and not by those of another age."

This story therefore comprises the history of Québec and Ontario. It includes the history in part of upstate New York, of France and of the Sulpicians and the Natives they encountered. It is a story of endurance, resolve, suffering, exploration and courage. Although recorded by the hand of a 17th Century Frenchman, it is the history of all of us including particularly the First Nations they encountered. History belongs to all of us as common property. To understand the past is to better understand the present.

The French version of the National Anthem of Canada describes our history as, "an epic of shining exploits," *une épopée des plus brillants exploits*. This story qualifies as one such "shining achievement". And if the reader should think that I am alone in this belief, I am reasonably certain that my friend *"Henri"* would agree.

John D. Ayre
September 2016
Norfolk, Ontario
Canada

HENRI'S STORY
Mes Rêves

My body is frail and I do not have a long time left on this earth. But my mind is calm and clear with what I saw and what I did. After our voyage to Lac Erié and the wintering there I was content to remain at Montréal and so I stayed there and I found a wife. Leaving the garrison, I obtained a farm at the west end of the Island of Montréal, a place called Lachine on lands owned by the good Sulpicians, lands that had once belonged to M. La Salle. Of him I later heard that he travelled much and travelled deep into the countryside. But then I heard no more.

In the year of 1689 our old enemies the Iroquois struck again and in such numbers we thought the world would end. My beloved wife died from a sickness she acquired while we sheltered from the Iroquois at the garrison in Montréal.

Of the other six men I paddled with some left for France after our voyage, some took on the life of the fur trade in Canada and of the others I do not know. My friend Thomàs remained in Canada. Père Galinée went back to France. I was told he died there. Père Dollier remained in Montréal and did the work of a Saint. I think of him often and smile. I never knew such men as Père Dollier and Galinée.

After the great Iroquois War ended in the Year of our Lord 1701, I returned to France after selling my small possessions and went to the place where I was born, to Blois on the River Loire where I relate this story to my blessed sister. My beloved France had been bled in wars with her neighbors while I was in New France. The countryside was poor. I was poor as I always had been, but I was rich in memories of a sort few men are privileged to possess.

The River Loire flows swiftly at Blois where I was born so long ago. I look at the river as if it is speaking to me about the passing of time of which I have but very little left. It reminds me always of the Rivers of Canada. When I sleep I often dream of the silence of the great forests where we hunted and of the cathedrals of trees of the place where we spent the winter. In my mind I hear the sound of the waters on the sides of our canoes as we paddled on, and forever on. I wonder if paradise is like this?

In my dreams there is both a terrifying silence and there are sounds that haunt me. The Iroquois told us that the forest and the lakes and the winds were possessed of Spirits that are real and speak to the souls of men and that these Spirits should be venerated.

Peut-être les Indiens ont eu raison.

Perhaps the Indians were right.

CHAPTER 17

The Untold Story

———

THEY CALL ME SIOUQORI. I am of the Onondowa'ga of the family of Hodinohso:ni, the people of the longhouse. The French called us Tsonnontouans. My people call me one of their elders...a wise man. I have seen many things and gone on many hunts. The Black Robes who are at our village now asked me to tell them the story of the two Black Robes who came here many years ago with many soldiers and a man named La Salle. The man La Salle came later and built a great canoe with white sails on the Lake of the Eries but of this I was only told. The French needed our help. We gave them help. Yet they destroyed our sacred stone at the end of the great lake. We prayed to the spirit of the stone to guide us in our journeys and they took it away. I do not understand why since it did them no harm. We are people. They do not understand the spirits of the forest. They do not try to understand us.

I was with a party of hunters who saw the Black Robes at their wintering place on the edge of the Lake of the Eries. We heard them singing and had no trouble finding the place with the tracks they left in the snow and the smoke coming from their shelter. We wanted to know if they were going to stay but we did not tell them that was why we were there. I was not recognised by the French having seen them before at our village Tinaoutoua for I was then a younger man of no importance.

Many years ago and many years after the Black Robes came to Tinaoutoua other French came with many soldiers to Ganondagan and burned all the villages. My son was taken prisoner near Montreal and sent to the land of the French as a captive to row their great canoes. I heard of this from his friend who was also sent to France but returned. My son did not return but died of a sickness on the great vessel.

I do not know what will become of my people. There are many French here and even more English below the lakes. They have guns and even canons that I have seen. Some are good. Some are not. They bring sickness sometimes to our people but say they can save our spirits. They baptize our sick who die anyway. Some of us wonder if the baptism makes them die. Others say it is not so. All the French want are furs but we have fewer furs each year. We shared with them the things we had. We taught them how to make and use our snowshoes so they could hunt and not starve in the winter. We taught them how to travel on the waters with our canoes.

Some of the French believe a man is strong because of how much wealth he gathers around him. We know a man's worth by what he shares with others.

I fear for my remaining children and their children. As for my people we must survive.

We will live on. That is all we can do.

Introduction

1. James Henry Coyne, FRSC (October 3, 1849 - January 5, 1942) was born in St. Thomas, Canada West (now Ontario). Coyne graduated from University College, Toronto in 1870. He studied law in St. Thomas and was called to the Ontario Bar in 1874. He practiced law in St. Thomas. From 1898 to 1902, he was President of the Ontario Historical Society and was appointed by Interior Minister and future Prime Minister Arthur Meighan as a member of the Historic Sites and Monuments Board of Canada from 1919 to 1930. He was a member of the Norfolk Historical Society. In 1906 he was made a Fellow of the Royal Society of Canada and served as its president from 1926 to 1927. Coyne was described by one contemporary as "an indefatigable historical miner of facts."

NOTES TO CHAPTER ONE. Historical Background

1. Slavery in New France had a long history dating back to Jacques Cartier who abducted several Natives and took them against their will to France. Its de facto existence was given a legal basis in 1709 by virtue of an Ordinance of the Intendant at Québec. It included both black slaves, however few in number and native slaves acquired by the French from other Natives who were universally referred to by the French as " *Panis* " a corruption of Puants or Winnebagos as they were also known.

2. The Nipissing were an Algonkian speaking band strategically living in the vicinity of the Mattawa River and the Lake that bears their name to this day and on whose shore the City of North Bay is located. Situated on the route to Huronia and the Sault, proximate to all of the northern bands and their fur-rich territories the Nipissing were uniquely positioned to derive whatever economic benefits they might from contact with the French. For their part, the French were wise to keep on friendly terms with the Nipissing. However nothing in the relationship would or could protect the Nipissing from the onslaught of diseases the French brought with them, against which they and most other Natives in North America had little immunity. In time they too would find their numbers significantly depleted from disease.

3. The source of information for the distance to be travelled and the description of the lands being "thickly populated" comes from Dollier's *History of Montréal*. Although he says very little about his voyage with Galinée, in fact only two pages worth he did offer a few morsels of information such as these.

4. The Récollets were in fact the first religious order to arrive in New France with Champlain. The Jesuits founded by Saint Ignatius Loyola were by 1669 far larger, better organised and better funded than any other Order. By the year 1669 the Jesuits already had a presence in India and China. New France was merely their latest extension. It would be the Jesuits who founded Ste. Marie among the Hurons and who had the greatest impact in Huronia until 1649 when the Iroquois attacked driving out the Huron and killing Jean de Brébeuf and Gabriel Lalement, both later canonised in the Twentieth Century.

5. The name" Huron" was a word of French construction as the Huron called themselves Wendat or Wyandotte meaning Islanders or People of the Peninsula. The Five Nations would become the Six Nations only in the early 1730's upon inviting the Tuscarora, an Iroquois speaking nation living to the south to join them. The Tuscarora's had been defeated and dispersed by colonists in their homelands that included western North Carolina. The Five Nations had joined together as a Confederacy only in the fifteenth or sixteenth century as a means to end the near constant wars that previously had existed between themselves.

6. In fact one European had traversed the Appalachians earlier. In 1540 the ruthless Hernando de Soto led his armed band from western North Carolina, across the mountains and into Tennessee before crossing the Mississippi where he died. De Soto would be followed by fellow Spaniard Juan Pardo in 1567. The bloody paths they cut through the Natives lands left no lasting legacy. Other Spanish had penetrated deeply into the American southwest throughout the sixteenth century but started from Mexico.

NOTES TO CHAPTER TWO. Genesis and Dollier de Casson

1. The Jesuit Relations were a series of letters written in New France, heavily edited by the Jesuits and published annually in France between 1632 and 1673.

2. Michael Barthélemy, born 1638 was a Sulpician priest who arrived in Canada in 1655. At the behest of Abbé de Queylus it was he who accompanied Dollier to the land of the Nipissing in the winter of 1668-1669 to learn their language. Replaced by Galinée, Barthélemy would in later years serve at the Sulpician's Kenté mission near present day Kingston, Ontario and as an accomplished linguist would serve the Algonkian community working with Dollier in Montréal. He would die there in 1706.

3. The first ships from France did not arrive in New France until the end of June 1669. While outfitting his expedition in May, Dollier would find that Montréal would not have had many of the necessary provisions he required as they would have been dispatched with the fur traders to the upper country as soon as the Ottawa River was ice free. Québec was by far a better suppled entrepôt for items to trade with the Natives, weapons etc.

4. Daniel de Remy de Courcelles (1626-1698) was appointed Governor General of New France in 1665 arriving at the same time as the first Intendant Jean Talon.

5. The "Neutrals "were an Iroquoian people who were outside of the Five Nations Confederacy. Living principally on the north shore of Lake Erie, they were in close trading contact with the Hurons. They were "Neutral "only vis à vis the French and hence the name. In fact, prior to their destruction they had been engaged in significant warfare with other Natives to the southwest.

6. The Jesuit Relations for 1641 reveals that Lake Erie was known by that name and also as lac des Chats or Lake of the Cat people as the Eries were known. The Neutral Iroquois further passed on to Chaumonot that Erie was fed by the fresh water sea, Lake Huron and that it emptied into *Onguiaahra* or Niagara, one of the few surviving Neutral words.

7. Although the terms voyageur and Coureurs de Bois or "Runners of the Woods" are often used interchangeably today there was a vast difference. The right to trade in furs with the Natives was strictly controlled by the Government of New France. Expensive licences were issued to engage in the fur trade and penalties for illegal trading were severe. The law was almost universally ignored and those who were engaged in the un-licenced trade were called Coureurs de Bois. It was a pejorative term. It may be said that anyone travelling was a voyageur. Those without a licence or official permission were Coureurs and if caught subject to fines and forfeiture or worse. As noted Dollier and LaSalle had the necessary travel permissions. If any Coureurs de Bois had seen Lake Erie, they weren't talking.

8. Margry at p. 290 names two of La Salle's companions as Le Sieur Charles Thoulonnier who was under a contract of engagement for which he was to be paid 400 Livres until October 20ᵗʰ, 1670. He also names one Sieur de La Roussillière as surgeon. All this cost fell to La Salle in addition to outfitting them with their canoes, their equipment and their necessities of life. This was very expensive for La Salle. La Rousillière would have been the first "surgeon "to enter modern Ontario. Most of the Companies of the Carignan Regiment had surgeons but their function, skill and training should not be confused with modern surgeons or Doctors.

NOTES TO CHAPTER FOUR. Departure & Ascent of the St. Lawrence

1. At this stage of their journey according to Galinée they also fished for Eel. Eel was a preferred food as salt water Eels from the Sargasso Sea in the Atlantic migrated up the St. Lawrence into Lake Ontario to breed. Eel provided a greater protein and caloric value for the men than did fresh water fish. Some suggest their migration is an artifact of the pre-glacial age.

2. In 1668 two Sulpician priests Abbé Claude Trouvé and Abbé Francois de Fénelon travelled to Prince Edward County in order to establish a Mission among the Iroquois at the Cayuga village of Kenté. The exact whereabouts of Kenté is unknown, although archaeological evidence suggests it was near the shore of Consecon Lake. The Cayuga there had asked for Black Robes to come to them as the presence of the Sulpicians provided a sort of guarantee against French attack. It was winter when the Priests arrived. Trouvé would make one visit to Tinoutoua at Dollier's written request. The small Sulpician mission of Kenté was largely unsuccessful, because "it cost a great deal to maintain and produced very little in return." In 1680 the Mission was abandoned. In fact Fénelon and fellow Sulpician M. Francois d'Urfé overwintered the same year as our travellers but at the mouth of the Rouge River to the east of modern Toronto. See also Endnote 1 Chapter 8.

NOTES TO CHAPTER FIVE. Canoes and Paddlers

1. Louis-Armand de Lom D'Arce de Lahontan (1666-circa 1716) spent approximately a decade in New France arriving in 1683. He came from a wealthy family in the south west of France and would write at length of his extensive travels to the interior of Canada by canoe. As a soldier he was engaged in several operations against the Iroquois.

He kept a Journal and upon his return to France, meeting financial hardship, he published *"Nouveaux Voyages dans L'Amérique Septentrionale"* a three volume work that would be published in several languages. He died in exile from France due to arrest warrants that had been issued for him in that Country.

NOTES TO CHAPTER SIX. Iroquois and Northern New York

1. Ganondagan, the Seneca Village is now a State Historic Site near Victor New York. Ganondagan was occupied by the Seneca until its total destruction by Denonville's large military force in 1687.

2. Wampum was not currency. It had its own meaning to the First Nations. It was rare. It was difficult to produce in quantity and quality depending on its availability. Most Wampum contained sea shells that could only be found on the Atlantic Coast of modern New England. Its exchange was performed to mark the seriousness of the event and the importance the giver placed on it. The Natives did not seek it out in battle or enslave others to get it. That attribute lay with Europeans in their quest for gold, an element that had no practical application whatsoever.

3. Dogs were the only animal domesticated by the Iroquois serving as companions, sentinels and ceremonial eating. It was the only food source Galinée complained about.

4. Galinée in fact wrote that the prisoner asked to see some of the *"Mistigouch."* Gabriel Sagard at p. 67 interprets this Iroquoian word to mean" canoes or boats of wood", a name given to the French by virtue of the design of their vessels.

5. Frontenac, a later Governor of New France would permit Natives allied to the French to torture to death their Native captives. In the 1680's another Governor of New France would not bother with the middle man and when soldiers under his command captured three Iroquois near Lac des Deux Montagnes he had the prisoners burned alive in the Place Royale in Montréal.

6. Source *Canadian Dictionary of Biography* Vol. 1 p. 173 and Robinson, P. *Toronto during the French Regime* p. 64. Note 3)

NOTES TO CHAPTER SEVEN. Head of the Lake and Jolliet

1. Galinée describes the Snakes as up to six or seven feet long, black and as thick as a man's arm. The likely candidate is the male Timber rattlesnake. Ontario's sole Twenty First Century resident rattlesnake is the Massasauga rattler which rarely grows more than a meter long and differs significantly in colour from the Timber Rattlesnake. But the average Timber Rattlesnake is four feet long with some modern examples reaching nearly six feet in length. Their bodies are quite stocky and thick. They were extirpated from Ontario by the end of the 19th Century but can still be found (although threatened) in upstate New York. Elizabeth Simcoe, wife of Upper Canada's first English Lt-Governor John Graves Simcoe, would have several experiences with Timber Rattlesnakes in the Niagara Peninsula and elsewhere as she noted in her diary entries written in the 1790's. She described them as five to six feet long, dark and ugly that made a whizzing sound when shaking their rattles. The Canadian Encyclopedic digest Volume II at XXXI states that the label "Iroquois " (Haudenosaunee as they called themselves) is a French corruption of the Algonkian name given the Iroquois literally Real Adders, or figuratively... Rattlesnakes.

2. The site of Tinaoutoua has not been located through archeology in modern times. This may be due to the fact that it was a smaller village without large palisades or post holes from the construction of the Longhouses. These post moulds are stained soils from the decomposed wood and provide the clue to modern archeologists to start digging. Nonetheless its general location is held to be in the vicinity of Westover, Ontario. Galinée described the three day portage of five leagues to get there through difficult country and that on their departure on October 1ˢᵗ they travelled 9 or 10 leagues in three days to the Grand River. Both Galinée's map of 1670 and a map by Pierre Raffeix dated 1688 (See Figure 15 in the text) show the location of the village, the latter map also showing the portage route and the newly built Fort Niagara. In an unpublished paper written in 1946 Woodhouse (see bibliography) sought to establish Dollier's precise route from the shore of Lake Ontario to Tinaoutoua.

NOTES TO CHAPTER EIGHT. Tinaoutoua and Descent of the Grand River

1. One source (Robinson) suggests that Jolliet took the shortest and easiest route to Huronia and then to Lake Superior by taking the eastern branch of the Toronto 'Carrying Place' route. This portage route led north from Lake Ontario either via the Rouge River, closest to Montréal or the Humber River and then to Lake Simcoe and into Georgian Bay. Hence he would have been familiar with the route from Montreal to the Rouge, just east of modern Toronto. A notation on Galinée's map marking the approximate position of the Rouge River tends to support this.

2. Galinée does not mention La Sotière by name in his Journal but, neither does he name any of his seven ex-soldier companions nor any of La Salle's party. When he counts the number of canoes departing Montréal he does not include the canoe with the Seneca guides among their number. Then again, Galinée's Journal was in the form of a report to Intendant Jean Talon and thence France and he would have included only that which he perceived to be essential. The source for La Sotière's name is Campeau at p. 21, see Bibliography. Margry also makes reference to a third person in Jolliet's canoe, likely the Native guide.

3. The first Catholic Mass in Ontario was likely celebrated in August 1615 by the Récollect Father Joseph Le Caron (born c. 1586 died 1632) in Huronia at the Huron Village of Carhagouha. See Bibliography Heidenreich. *A New Location for Carhagouha, Recollect Mission in Huronia.*

4. Galinée makes reference to having sails for their canoes. These were very simple sheets of cloth that could be used as an aid to paddling but only when the wind was from astern and only when the water was relatively calm.

5. Galinée wrote a letter to de Fénelon at Kenté. By November 1670 and possibly even November 1669 Trouvé would arrive in Tinaoutoua. It is possible Jolliet or La Salle carried the letter back to Kenté or in any event to Montréal. Evidently Galinée had writing paper and ink which may suggest he made writings during the journey later reduced into the comprehensive Journal. Since Trouvé's comments about being able to hear Niagara Falls from Burlington Bay were included in the Journal that was sent to France in late 1670, Galinée must have heard this from Trouvé after his arrival back in Montreal.

6. Given Galinée's repeated assertion that he was more "used" to Maritime charts than others, I have assumed he preferred and used the Maritime League being the equivalent of 3.45 miles or 5.5 kilometers. As there was no standard

league in use in France at the time there were other shorter Leagues. Common leagues and Legal Leagues were in use in France, both of which were shorter than the Maritime League. Sixty years earlier, Champlain, an expert cartographer for his time, would use different leagues at different times on the same map.

NOTES TO CHAPTER NINE. The Over Wintering of 1669-1670 at Port Dover

1. In the early 1880's a local Norfolk Resident, one Thomas Jackson of Woodhouse found a broken axe head about two kilometers from the wintering site. Walker (see bibliography) noted it changed hands until 1915. Its type and markings were consistent with the axes used by the French of the era and could have been one of the expeditions axes that broke, as Galinée complained they frequently did, due to the cold. Or it could have been an axe simply traded to the Natives at some undetermined time. The axe was subsequently lost, allegedly after it was sent for examination to a museum out of Province.

2. Fischer, D.H. (see bibliography at p. 630 describes) a *barrique* as representing a volume in well in excess of two hundred litres. The Récollet Priest Gabriel Sagard in his 1632 book, *Le Grand Voyage du Pays des Hurons* described that during his journey into Huronia in 1623 and having exhausted their supply of sacramental wine they were obliged to use local grapes and filled a small barrel and two small bottles with wine they made in that location that proved sufficient for their purposes. He did not, like Galinée, extoll or compare its virtues to the wines of France nor did he produce anything like the quantity Dollier appears to have made.

3. Although there is no direct evidence of what they stored their wine in it is completely unlikely that they had bottles in their canoes and less so that they would have used empty gunpowder casks. Properly cleaned out the bladders of the deer they had shot and particularly stag bladders, (being easier to remove intact from the carcass) would have served the purpose once washed out in the ample fresh water available. A modern application in the field of what is called "biodynamic wine making" still seems to include the use of stag bladder. Dollier may have had <u>some</u> limited traditional means to store wine, such as a cask since they celebrated Mass at Tinaoutoua and their only source of sacramental wine until arrival at the Wintering Site would have been what they brought from Montréal.

NOTES TO CHAPTER TEN. Food and Provisions

1. My thanks to Eric Fernberg, Collections specialist, Canadian War Museum on this subject. Further analysis of the history of firearms available to the French can be found in *Le Peuple, L'Etat et la Guerre au Canada sous le Régime Francais* by Louise Dechêne, Boréal 2008 at p. 535 and also Fischer p. 616 with respect to weaponry in Champlain's time.

NOTES TO CHAPTER ELEVEN. Exodus: Spring 1670

1. Henri de Tonty (1650-1704) was an Italian born soldier-adventurer -explorer who served firstly in the French Navy when he had his right hand shot off during an attack against the Spanish in Sicily. He served in Canada as La Salle's principal agent and travelled all of New France from Québec to Louisiana. On at least one occasion in 1678 he traversed the north shore of Lake Erie and at the very least would have passed the wintering site and Long Point. He was engaged in numerous battles with and against Natives as circumstances dictated. His life story could be the subject of its own adventure film.

2. In 1613 Champlain had done something similar during his ascent of the Ottawa River at Allumette Island when he raised a Cross bearing the Coat of Arms of France as had Jacques Cartier at Gaspé approximately eighty years before.

3. Unbeknownst to Dollier, Pope Clement IX had died a few months before on December 9th, 1669 while they were encamped at the Wintering Site. He was succeeded by Pope Clement X, (elected April 29th and crowned May 11th, 1670) who would read of the explorations occurring in New France, including Dollier's and in some degree this was a factor in his decision to create a Bishopric in Québec, first held by Francois de Laval. Laval was canonized by Pope Francis in 2014.

4. The four creeks west of the Turkey Point Marsh are Mud Creek, Dedrick's Creek, Big Creek and Clear Creek.

5. In his *History of Montreal* Dollier noted that their departure in July 1669 from that future City had been delayed not three days as Galinée asserted but 15 days. If this is accurate then but for the murder of the Seneca, the apprehension of the offenders and their execution, Dollier might have left without Galinée and in the company of Bartholémy. In any event it appears Galinée had but three days to get ready.

6. This writer's earlier training as a prosecutor caused me to consider a skeptic's theory that perhaps the two men sent out by Dollier to locate Jolliet's canoe in the autumn of 1669 had not in fact done so, contrary to what they had reported. The men were not accompanied by either Dollier or Galinée. Their eight day journey to Port Stanley (if that is where the canoe was) and their return to Port Dover was very fast if made by canoe assuming good weather conditions and impossibly fast if they went by land to that location. It seems curious that someone else would have found the canoe and not destroyed it or even left it where it was, but moved it a relatively short distance away, such that however well concealed it was it could be found again. That third party's effort would also include the need to conceal it again and in such a fashion that it would be preserved from the winter elements.

   Soldiers of all eras are good at self-preservation and the avoidance of unnecessary harm and it might have been tempting for the two soldiers to report that they had found the canoe (which at that point they did not require) and return to the Wintering Site, knowing that they could later say, if necessary, that it had been moved by others. But since this skeptic's approach lies in theory only without supporting evidence, we will mention it no further.

NOTE TO CHAPTER TWELVE. Disaster at Point Pelée

1. In his *History of Montréal* Dollier defined the Chapel Set (sa chapelle) as " Le nécessaire pour dire la messe ". In other words more than merely a chalice.

NOTES TO CHAPTER THIRTEEN. Sault Ste. Marie and Return to Montréal

1. France would lose Acadia once again and for the final time to the English in 1714 after yet another of Louis XIV's wars. They would keep Isle Royale or Cape Breton until the destruction of Louisbourg by the British in 1758.

2. Tertian Fever is so called because the symptoms of fever, chills shivering and vomiting would arise every three days. It was later called ague, or marsh fever until the modern nomenclature Malaria was adopted." Malaria" derives

from the Italian Mal-Aria or bad air. Malaria has different forms but it is a parasite that invades human red blood cells and is transmitted to humans by mosquitos. Symptoms arise within a few weeks of infection hence Galinée likely contracted it during those last few weeks of the voyage. It was endemic to North America well into the 19th century and remains so in large parts of the world.

NOTES TO CHAPTER FIFTEEN. Dénouement

1. One of La Salle's ships from the ill-fated Texas expedition *La Belle* was wrecked in 1686 at Matagorda Bay Texas and recovered there in the 1990's. Relics from the vessel are on display in that State under the auspices of the Texas Historical Commission.

2. Departing La Rochelle on July 12th, 1678 on the vessel Saint-Honoré, with Dollier and La Salle was Henri de Tonty, about to embark on his North American adventures. See Endnote 1 for Chapter 11.

In Port Dover, Ontario there are two historical sites marking and commemorating the location of the Wintering Site. The first and least controversial is the Cross of Dollier and Galinée which stands on a plinth on Brown Street near the end of Brant Hill Road. The two attached plaques repeat in English and French the text of the Procès Verbal referred to in Chapter 11. Two other plaques also in French and English have this to say…

"Near this spot, March 23rd, 1670, was erected a cross with arms of France and inscription claiming sovereignty in the name of King Louis XIV over the Lake Erie region, as shown in procès-verbal reproduced on this memorial placed here in 1922. Canada was ceded by France to Great Britain in 1763."

It is correct to state that the lovely cross overlooking the waters of Lake Erie was placed "near the spot" and not <u>on</u> the spot. This is true for two reasons. Firstly, Galinée did not specify the precise location other than to say *On the 23rd of March, Passion Sunday we all went to the lake shore to make and plant a Cross in memory of so long a long sojourn (d'une si longue demeure des Francois, comme avaoit esté la nostre) as ours had been*"(From Galinée's Journal).

The second reason is that the lake shore of 1670 would have been quite different from its modern configuration. The shores of Lake Erie are notoriously subject to erosion. The shoreline west of Long Point is the most severely eroded and continues to erode. So the current plaque, marker and Cross are correct…it was "nearby" that the Procès Verbal was posted and as we have seen it would have been placed in a sufficiently conspicuous location that it would need to stand only long enough for the Iroquois to find it before it fell down due to the elements. Finally, succumbing to urban growth, the original Cross marker of 1922 was moved in 1953 from its placement site to its current location to accommodate road expansion.

The second historical plaque in Port Dover is on a Stone Cairn marked as a National Historic Site and is somewhat more controversial. James Coyne and others were adamant that this was the precise location of the over wintering site and with the weight of the Norfolk Historical Society and others saw that it was so designated in 1922. It came to pass that shortly after Canada's 1967 Centennial the Federal Government sought to de-designate it, an act that was opposed locally with equal vigour as that which existed to have it initially designated. The Cairn is just off Donjon Blvd in Port Dover in a ravine that slopes down to Black Creek.

The legal description is part of Lot 13, Concession 1, Township of Woodhouse, measuring 0.053 hectares (0.132 acres). This parcel of land is on the south bank of Black Creek, Port Dover, and was acquired by the Crown in 1922.

There is a pleasant fenced area protecting some mounds which are held out as evidence of the Frenchmen's sojourn there. On either side of the site, to the east and west there are modern residences at the top of the sides of the ravine. The plaque on this Cairn reads…

"Historic Sites and Monuments Board of Canada.

Here, 1669-1670, wintered Dollier and Galinée with seven other Frenchmen, the first Europeans known to have ascended the Great Lakes to Sault Ste. Marie. The earthen mounds are the remains of their hut, which was at once residence, chapel and fort."

Or was it so? In 1967 Parks Canada commissioned an excavation of the site which work was conducted under the auspices of a very experienced archeologist Iaian C. Walker (1938-1984). He concluded his detailed analysis with the observation that *"the archeological evidence produced no positive evidence to authenticate the site, and has produced indirect evidence that the site is not that of the wintering".* (Walker p.30 see bibliography). As a lawyer and the author of this text I wish to venture my own opinion both with respect to the site, the mounds and Walker's Report.

Figure 26. Photo of the Wintering Site Cairn in Port Dover.

Walker noted that the site had been excavated by both professionals and amateurs over the years. Site contamination might be the best word to describe what had happened to the area as objects from the Twentieth Century were found there. The stream that flows through the site down the ravine, has been diverted. A railway had been built in the 19th Century and likely ran right along the southern ridge where one now parks their car to descend the stairs to the site of the Cairn. That creek and his soil analysis told Walker that it would not be a likely spot to build what Galinée called *"une fort bonne cabane "* a strong good cabin of a type built so that they could have defended themselves for long time against the Natives if they had attacked *'Aussi l'avions-nous bastie de sorte que nous eussions pu nous défendre longtemps contre ces barbares, s'ils leur eust pris envie de nous venir faire insulte.'*

The Historic Sites and Monuments Board of Parks Canada has had the issue of the precise location of the wintering site and the wording on the Cairn come before it on a number of occasions, beginning in 1947 and again in the period of 1983-1989 with the last such report being filed in 2008. Issues arose before that body of de-designating the site or rewording the plaque.

Consider that Dollier's cabin was built to last only over one winter season. Unlike ancient Iroquois Longhouse villages, one could not necessarily expect to find posthole markers centuries later as are often identifiable in the case of much larger native villages, which were often built to be occupied for a decade or even much longer.

As for the mounds on the site, Walker conducted detailed and scientific analysis of the soil and could only say that they had likely been a "dump" for soil suggestive of the use of a wheelbarrow, something not carried in the canoes by our adventurers. Walker accepted fully that the ravine and Cairn are in the general area and even posited that it may have been at the top of the ravine on the east or west side of where the cairn is positioned. I tend to agree but perhaps for other reasons.

There was a strong local oral history dating back to the late eighteenth century that the site was connected with the French. There were artifacts found in the area from the Eighteenth Century including a broken French axe head of the right approximate age. Recalling that Galinée complained about the axes breaking it is a shame that Coyne and others reported that the axe head had been lost by the museum to which it was sent (see Endnote 1 for Chapter 9).

Walker's team found a clay pipe nearby which was also "taken out of storage and lost "according to Walker. He himself had a particular interest in historical clay pipes as markers by which to time human occupation and had written previously on the subject. There were no other significant artifacts found to fix the precise site. Walker dismissed earlier advocates who said that the site was further down river. Subsequent French maps even into the mid seventeenth century describe the river as the place of the over wintering and Walker and Coyne (and this writer) are convinced that it was above the forks of the Lynn and Black Creek (also known as Patterson's Creek).

Perhaps the error, if it is an error on the part of Walker is that he was looking for incontrovertible physical proof of the presence of the Sulpicians. But that of course was his job. He was looking to confirm the site by what I would call in my earlier career, "proof beyond a reasonable doubt."

If one applies a lesser standard, the balance of probabilities, or the preponderance of evidence, then what?

I have canoed up the Creek past the Wintering Site. I have looked at aerial photos. Consider what we know. The cabin was large enough for all nine men and their provisions. They would need to store their fairly bountiful food provisions, cook and pray at their Altar. Of necessity they would have had a fire pit for heat and cooking. They needed fresh water to be available from the river even when iced over. They needed to store their weapons and all other articles.

Further, what of their canoes? The three canoes were almost as important to them as their very lives. The present visible mounds at the site are simply too small for such a structure. And why if they feared being attacked would they build their defensible structure at the bottom of a hill? I do not believe that with his military training and wilderness experience Dollier would have done so. They might have built a structure in the ravine to protect their canoes. But the "mounds" do not represent a structure large enough to hold three twenty foot canoes, all their provisions, all the while permitting the men to defend themselves for a long time if need be. In Chapter Two the writer introduced the reader to the 1632 publication of the Récollet Gabriel Sagard whose work Dollier may have read. He described the winter habitation that he built and shared with two other Priests (and not while burdened with three canoes) as about twenty feet long and ten or twelve wide made in the form of a garden bower, covered all over with bark including the roof except an opening for the smoke. They made two rooms in the structure, one for sleeping and eating and the other as a small chapel for the performance of Mass. It may have served as a model for Dollier along with the other smaller native huts he had seen himself.

There is no other site on the creek that would permit a strong defensive position while protecting the canoes from the elements than the current site, but with the "cabane" on the east or west side at the top of the ravine. If one removes from the equation the mounds that are visible on the site, all of the other indicators still point favourably to the "general" location as that of the Wintering Site.

It is perhaps therefore sufficient to say that the currently marked site was likely part of their world as they over wintered. They would have traveled up and down the shoreline to hunt and penetrated the woods to the north in the general direction of the modern town of Simcoe, limited only by the depth of the snow, availability of game and their ability to take back to their site what they had killed. Which Wintering Site, we may be sure on balance, was within the "environs "of the Cairn erected in 1922 to mark the visit of Dollier and Galinée.

And those are my submissions on the subject.

(~ indicates approximate date)

1668
Dollier spends part of the winter among the Nipissing.

1669
July 3 Galinée selected to take the place of Bartholémy and begins his preparations.

July 6 Departure of Dollier, Galinée and La Salle from Montréal.

August 2 Arrival at Lake Ontario.

August 8 Arrival at Oswego and the River of the Onondaga.

August 10 Arrival at Irondequoit Bay.

August 12 Leaving Dollier on the shore Galinée, La Salle and eight Frenchmen head inland to the Ganondagan.

August 13 Galinée and La Salle meet the assembled Elders at Ganondagan.

August 14 The meeting with the Elders continues as they present wampum to the French. The Seneca state it should be no more than a week for the necessary guide to arrive.

~ August 21 Galinée and La Salle visit the Bitumen springs

August 26 Galinée records the latitude at Karontagouat (Irondequoit, New York) east of Genesee river as 43 Degrees 12 Minutes N. Lat.

September 19 For three days Dollier waits at Burlington Bay at or near present day La Salle Park.

September 22 Dollier and company set out from the shore of Lake Ontario to Tinaoutoua.

September 23 The portage to Tinaoutoua continues with native help. The French learn of Jolliet's presence there.

September 24 Arrival at Tinaoutoua and meeting Jolliet.

September 30 Mass is said at Tinaoutoua with La Salle still present.

October 1 Dollier leaves Tinaoutoua and commence portage to the Grand River. La Salle departs.

October 3 Saint Francis' day Dollier arrives at the Grand River and Mass is said on its banks.

October 3 The Dutchman and two natives set out to find place of Jolliet's canoe.

October 4 The French begin the descent of the Grand River.

October 13/14 They arrive at mouth of Grand and see Lake Erie for the first time.

~ October 17 Arrival at Port Dover.

~October 17 Two of the soldiers are sent to find Jolliet's Canoe.

~October 25 The two men return reporting they found the canoe but not the Dutchman.

~October 28 – November 1 after two weeks on the shore awaiting possible arrival of the Dutchman Dollier moves his party a quarter of a league up the river to the Wintering Site.

1670
~ February 1 After three months of solitude the Iroquois come upon the Wintering Site.

March 23 On Passion Sunday a Cross is planted at the lake shore, Mass is celebrated and the Procès-Verbal is read out.

March 26 Dollier and party depart Port Dover.

~March 29 Turkey Point and Galinée's canoe is lost.

~March 30 The five men travelling by land cross Big Creek in a raft.

April 1 They arrive on the shore of Lake Erie at the neck of Long Point.

April 2 The five land bound men rejoin the other four men in the two canoes.

April 6 The French celebrate Easter of 1670 at Long Point shore line while resting.

~ April 11 They arrive at Port Stanley later known as Riviére Tonti.

May 25 Arrival at Sault Ste. Marie.

May 28 Departure from the Jesuit Mission at Sault Ste. Marie.

June 18 Arrival of the nine men at Montréal.

June-September The Journal is finalised and sent by ship to France along with a copy of the Procs Verbal and the first version of Galinée's Map.

November Intendant Jean Talon dispatches another vessel to France containing a second version of the Map with additions from Trouvé and Fénelon.

ILLUSTRATIONS

ILLUSTRATIONS FROM CODEX CANADENSIS ARE Public Domain, Courtesy of the Gilcrease Museum of Tulsa, OK, and Library and Archives Canada. All others are public domain or by the author or as cited.

1. Early Map of Montreal
2. Champlain. Self-portrait firing arquebus
3. Louis XIV painting by Rigaud
4. Warrior from *Codex Canadensis*
5. Champlain's 1632 map
6. Sanson 1650 map
7. Canadien soldier on snowshoes
8. La Salle
9. Voyageurs at Dawn painting by Hopkins
10. Jacobs staff
11. Lahontan canoes
12. Mahican village with Longhouses
13. Plan of forts showing Ganondagan
14. Site of Burning Spring Bristol. N.Y.
15. Site of Ganondagan. Victor N.Y.
16. Raffeix map of 1688 showing Tinaoutoua
17. Rattlesnake from *Codex Canadensis*
18. Wintering Site by satellite
19. Procès Verbal in Dollier's handwriting
20. Lake St. Clair
21. Supplies at Sault Ste. Marie
22. French River painting by Paul Kane
23. Galinée's map
24. Dollier in later years
25. Sulpician Seminary Montréal
26. Wintering Site Cairn, Port Dover

BIBLIOGRAPHY

Arbic, Bernie *City of the Rapids: Sault Ste. Marie's Heritage* Priscilla Press, Michigan 2003

Bamford, Paul Walden. *The Procurement of Oarsmen for French Galleys, 1660-1748* The American Historical Review Vol. 65, No. 1 (October 1959) pp. 31-48

Baskerville, Peter A. *Ontario: Image, Identity and Power* Oxford University Press. 2002

Berthiaume, Pierre *Cavelier de la Salle Une Épopée aux Amériques Cosmopoles* 2006

Campeau, Lucien, s.j. S.R.C. *La découverte du lac Erié.* Les Cahiers des dix, no. 44, 1989, p.21-37

Casson, Dollier de *A History of Montréal* Ralph Flenley ed, and Translator J. M. Dent & Sons New York 1928

Champlain Society *The French Regime in the Upper Country of Canada during the Seventeenth Century.* Toronto Champlain Society 1996. University of Toronto Press

Clement, Daniel ed. *The Algonquins* Mercury Series Canadian Ethnology Service Paper 130 Canadian Museum of Civilisation 1996

Coyne, James H. Editor and translator *Exploration of the Great Lakes 1669-1670 Dollier de Casson and De Bréhant de Galinée* Ontario Historical Society Papers and Records Volume IV 1903.

Coyne, James H *The Dollier-Galinée Expedition 1669-1670.* Address given at Port Dover at unveiling of Memorial July 5th, 1922 Norfolk Public Library. Canadiana.

Croft, David J.A. *Champlain's Portage from Muskrat Lake to the Ottawa River.* Ontario Archaeology number 81/82 2006 pp 3-12

Cruikshank, Brigadier General E.A. *The Exploring Expedition of Dollier and Galinée in 1669-1670* Address given at Unveiling of Memorial Brant Hill Port Dover July 5, 1922 Norfolk Public Library. Canadiana.

Dechêne, Louise *Habitants and Merchants in Seventeenth Century Montréal.* McGill-Queens University Press 1992.

De Brumath, A. Leblond *Bishop Laval The Makers of Canada* Parkman Edition Volume II 1906. Morang & Co. Toronto.

Douville, Raymond. S.R.C. *Vie et mort d'Adrien Jolliet.* Les Cahiers des dix, no. 42, 1979, p.25-47.

Durant, Will and Ariel. *The Story of Civilization: Part VIII The Age of Louis XIV* Simon and Schuster New York 1963.

Eccles, W.J. Denonville et les galériens Iroquois. Revue d'histoire de l'Amérique francaise, vol. 14, No. 3, 1960, p. 408-429.

Eccles, W.J. *Canada under Louis XIV 1663-1701* The Canadian Centenary Series McClelland and Stewart 1964.

Eccles, W.J. *The French in North America* 1500-1783 Fitzhenry & Whiteside 1998.

Englebert, Robert and Teasdale, Guillame *French and Indians in the Heart of North America 1630-1815.* Michigan State University Press and University of Manitoba Press 2013.

Dictionary of Canadian Biography Volume I 1000-1700 and Volume II, 1701-1740. University of Toronto Press. 1969. David M Hayne editor.

Faillon, Etienne Michel. *Histoire de la Colonie Francaise en Canada Vol 3 Bibliothèque Paroissiale Paris 1866.*

Finkelstein, Maxwell W. *Canoeing a Continent On the Trail of Alexander Mackenzie* Natural Heritage Books 2002 Toronto

Fischer, David Hackett *Champlain's Dream* Alfred A. Knopf Canada 2008.

Gagnon, Louis *Louis XIV et le Canada* 1658-1674 Septentrion.

Gold Thwaites, Reuben ed. *The Jesuit Relations and allied Documents: Travels and Explorations of the Jesuit Missionaries in New France, 1610-1791,* 73 vols. Cleveland: Burrows Brothers, 1896-1903.

Grady, Wayne *The Great Lakes: The Natural History of a Changing Region.* Greystone Books Toronto 2007.

Hayes, Derek *Historical Atlas of Canada* Douglas and McIntyre 2006.

Heidenreich, Conrad E. *A New location for Carhagouha, Recollect Mission in Huronia.* Abstract 1967.

Heidenreich, Conrad E. *Explorations and Mapping of Samuel de Champlain, 1603-1632.* Cartographica Monograph No. 17/1976.

Huck, Barbara *Exploring the Fur Trade Routes of North America* Heartland. Winnipeg 2012.

Index and Dictionary of Canadian History. Lawrence J. Burpee ed. 1911 Toronto Morang and Co.

Jaenen, Cornelius J. *The French Regime in the Upper Country of Canada during the Seventeenth Century.* Toronto. Champlain Society 1996.

Jennings, Francis *The Ambiguous Iroquois Empire* W.W. Norton & Co. N.Y. 1984.

Johnston, Charles M. ed. The Valley of the Six Nations: A Collection of Documents on the Indian Lands of the Grand River. Champlain Society University of Toronto Press 1964.

LaFrance, Marc *De la Qualité des Vins en Nouvelle-France.* Cap-aux-Diamants: la revue d'histoire du Québec, No. 28, 1992, p 14-17.

Lanctot, Gustave. *A History of Canada Volume Two: From the Royal Regime to the Treaty of Utrecht, 1663-1713* Clarke, Irwin & Co. Toronto 1964.

Lahontan, Baron *New Voyages to North America 1703* reprinted 1905 R.G. Thwaites McClung & Co. Chicago.

Les Prêtres de Saint-Sulpice au Canada: Grandes Figures de leur Histoire University of Laval Press Sainte-Foy 1992.

Les Sulpiciens de Montréal: Une Histoire de Pouvoir et de Discrétion 1657-2007. Delandres, Dickinson and Hubert eds. Fides 2007.

The Lake Erie Cross : A Brief Record Department of the Interior. Kings Printer Ottawa 1922.

Mackenzie, Sir Alexander. *The Journals of Alexander Mackenzie* Narrative Press 2001.

Mann, Charles C. *1493: Uncovering the New World Columbus Created* Alfred Knopf 2011.

Marchand, Phillip *Ghost Empire: How the French almost Conquered North America* McClelland & Stewart. Toronto 2006.

Margenton, Margaret F. *History of the Wintering Site* 1669-1670 Collection of the Norfolk Historical Society.

Marit K.Munson and Susan M.Jamieson editors *Before Ontario. The Archeology of a Province.* McGill-Queens University Press. 2013.

Marmier, Jean. *Le Récit de M. de Courcelle au Lac Ontario(1671) et Dollier de Casson* Révue d'histoire de l'Amérique francaise, vol 32, no. 2, 1978, p.239-250.

Marshall, Orasmus Holmes *The First Visit of de la Salle to the Seneca's in 1669* Buffalo N.Y. 1874.

Miquelon, Dale. *New France 1701-1744: A Supplement to Europe* McLelland and Stewart 1987

Morse, Eric W. *Fur Trade Routes of Canada: Then and Now* University of Toronto Press 1969.

Morse, Eric W. *Fur Trade Canoe Routes of Canada/ Then and Now* University of Toronto Press Toronto 1969 reprinted 1971 Oxford University Press 1964.

Munson, Marit K and Jamieson, Susan M editors *Before Ontario: The Archeology of a Province* McGill-Queens University Press 2013.

Nute, Grace Lee *The Voyageur* Minnesota Historical Press Society 1931 D. Appleton & Co.

Paradis, Jean Marc *Le Lieu de L'Hivernement de l'Expédition Dollier-Galinée 1669-1670.* Unpublished Thesis. Université Laval 1967.

Parkman, Francis *The Jesuits in North America in the Seventeenth Century :A Series of Historical Narratives* Part Second Boston Little, Brown & Co. 1884.

Parkman, Francis *The Old Regime in Canada* 14th edition Boston. Little Brown & Co. 1884 reprinted 1987.

Parks Canada: Historic Sites and Monuments Board of Canada. *Report to Clarify the Status of the Wintering Site National Historic Site* Report No. 2008-CED-SDC-45.

Parks Canada: Historic Sites and Monuments Board of Canada. *Report to Confirm the Designated Place of Cliff Site National Historic Site of Canada* Report No. 2008-CED-SDC-44.

Pearce, Bruce *Historical Highlights of Norfolk County* Vol. 1 Pearce Publishing co. 1967 and Vol. 2 Griffin and Richmond Co. Hamilton 1973.

Picton Gazette. *The Kenté Mission 1668-1680* Picton Gazette Publishing Co. 1968.

Podruchny, Carolyn *Making the Voyageur World: Travellers and Traders in the North American Fur Trade* University of Toronto Press 2006.

Riley, John L. *The Once and Future Great Lakes Country: An Ecological History.* McGill-Queens University Press 2013.

Robinson, Percy J. *Toronto during the French Regime.* 2nd edition University of Toronto Press. 1965.

Steckley, John L. *Words of the Huron* Wilfred Laurier Press 2007.

Soll, Jacob *The Information Master: Jean-Baptiste Colbert's Secret Intelligence System* University of Michigan Press 2011.

Thomson, Don W. *Men and Meridians:The History of Surveying and Mapping in Canada Volume I Prior to 1867.* Queens Printer, Ottawa 1967.

Trigger, Bruce G. *Natives and Newcomers: Canada's 'Heroic Age' Reconsidered*. McGill-Queens University Press. 1985.

Trudel, Marcel. *The Beginnings of New France 1524-1663* McClelland and Stewart 1973

Trudel, Marcel. *La Population du Canada en 1666*. Septentrion 1995.

Trudel, Marcel. *Canada's Forgotten Slaves: Two Hundred Years of Bondage* Véhicule Press 2013.

Verney, Jack *The Good Regiment:The Carignan-Salières Regiment in Canada 1665-1668* McGill-Queens University Press Montréal and Kingston 1991.

The Valley of the Six Nations: A Collection of Documents on the Indian Lands of the Grand River. Charles M. Johnston ed. The Champlain Society for the Government of Ontario. University of Toronto Press.

Walker, Iaian C. *Excavations at the Alleged Wintering Place of Dollier and Galinée in 1669-1670 at Port Dover, Ontario 1966*. Parks Canada 1967.

Richard White, *The Middle Ground: Indians, Empires, and Republics in the Great Lakes Region, 1650-1815* (New York: Cambridge University Press, 1991), 144; cf. 421.

Woodhouse, Roy T. *Route of La Salle and Galinée to Tinaoutoua*. Unpublished Manuscript, Hamilton Public Library 1946.

INDEX

Albany. N.Y. see Fort Orange
Andaste 6,48

Barthélemy, Michael 17, 20,96
Brébeuf, Jean 13,15,70,87
Bristol, N.Y. 38,111...bitumin spring
Brûlé, Etienne 13,50, 77
Burlington, Ontario 42,61,99,107

Cadillac, Antoine 73
Canandaigua, N.Y. 37
Canoes see Chapter Five, Canoes and Paddlers 29
Carignan-Salières Regiment 7,12,36, 58,86,97,117
Cartier, Jacques 7,33,55,59, 95,101
Champlain, Samuel xiv 3-5,13-15,
    57,59,60,65,72,77,96,100,101,111-114,115,117
Chaumonot, Pierre Joseph 13,15, 34,97
Clement IX...see Popes
Clement X...see Popes
Colbert, Jean Baptiste xiv,4,43,47,59,62,63-65,
    83-86,116
Courcelle, Daniel de Rémy 11-16,
    20-22,25,37,43,46-47,54,58,62-65,80,85-86
Coureurs de Bois 14,31,64,97
Coyne, James xiii,xiv,48,61,83,95,103,105,115
Cross, Lake Erie 62-65,103,108

Dablon, Claude 77
Denonville, Jacques-René 87,98,114
De Queylus, Gabriel 1, 9-11,
    15,17,18,21-22,79,81,86,88,92,96
Dollard, Adam 6

Dollier, Francois, birth and early years 10, arrive Canada
    11, 1666 Campaign 12,Nipissing guide 15,beginning
    of voyage 23, at Burlington 42,at Tinaoutoua 47,
    at Grand River 49,at Lake Erie 50,depart Port Dover
    61,at Point Pelée 70, after 1670 85, achievements in
    Montréal, death 90
D'Urfé, Francois 97

Faillon, Etienne-Michel xiii,114
Fénelon, Francois 83,85,97,99,109
Firearms 58,100
Five Nations (see also Seneca and Mohawk) 3-4,25,36,96
Food see Chapter Ten Food & Provisions 57
Fort Orange 4-5,15, 37-38,92
Frémin, Jacques 36-39,87,92
Frontenac, Louis 21,49,86,88,98

Galinée, René Bréhant ,Instructions 20, arrival in
    Canada 21,skills 21, at Ganondagan 34, description
    of food at wintering site 57,malaria 79, map 81 et
    seq.,journal 83, return to France and death 88
Ganastogué 40
Ganondagan 26,27,33-38,40,43,48,68,72,86-87,
    90,92,94,98,107,111,121
Grand River 13,44,47,49-50,71,82,90,99,108

Handsome Lake xv
Hennepin, Louis 42,86
Hudson, Henry 5,33
Hunting of Arthur 66-67,71
Huron and Huronia 3-4,13-14,40,95-96,
    99-100,116

Jacob's Staff 26-27,72, 81,111
Jesuits15-16 in New York 25,36, at SS Marie 75, 87, and Récollets 96-97
Jolliet,Adrien xiv,45-51,54,61-62,66-69,72-73, 83-85,92,98-99,101,108,114
Jolliet,Louis 47,61,77,91

Kenté Sulpician mission 25,40,49,72, 80,85-87,96-99

Lahontan, Louis-Amand xiv,29-32,97,111,115
Lake St. Clair & St.Clair River 32,48,73-74,84,111
La Roussillière, Sieur de, 97
La Salle Jean 11,21,86
La Salle, René Robert Sieur de …purpose 16, biographical details arrive Canada 21, at Ganondagan 34,at Burlington 42,at Tinaoutoua 47,return to Montréal 49,route to Montréal 85 and later trips, death 86
La Sotière 47,99
Laval, Bishop Francois 9,17-18,86,101
Leagues as a unit of measurement 70,83,99-100
LeCaron, Joseph 195
Long Point 50,53,56, 62,65-78,82,86,103,108-109
Louis XIV 4,7,9,12,16-17,62-65,79,81,84,87-88,103

Mackenzie, Alexander 77,114-115
Maisonneuve, Paul de Chomedy 4,9
Malaria (Tertian Fever) 79,84,101-102
Margry, Pierre xiii, 63,97,99
Marquette, Jacques 77,85,87,91
Ménard, René 6
Mohawk Nation 4-5,12-13,25,43,63,86
Montréal as *Ville Marie* xv, established 4, population 6, and Sulpicians 9, Dollier's *Histoire de Montréal* 11,17,23,83, attacks on 12,87 seminary 62, Dollier's contributions to 88-91

Neutral Iroquois 4,13,40, 96-97
Niagara 4,42-43,48,59,97,99
Nicollet, Jean 6
Nipissing 1,2,10-11,15,21,26,54-60,95-96
Nitarikyk 1,9,11,23,50,92

Olier, Jean-Jacques 9
Ottawa Nation xiv,xv,6,9,47-48,76,80,85

Peré, Jean 47
Point Peleé 70 et seq.
Popes…. Clement IX 62,101 and Clement X 101
Port Dover, (see also Wintering Site) xiv,xv, 50-55, 58,59,60-63,66,72,82,84,86,90,100-101, 103-104, 108,111
Port Stanley xv,48,61-62,91, 101,109
Potawatomi Nation xiv,6,48,62,67,91
Procès Verbal 62-64,81-84,103,108

Raffeix, Pierre 44,99,111
Rattlesnakes 43,45,98,111
Récollets 2,14-16,18,42,86-87,89,96,100,105

Sagamite 56,68
Sagard, Gabriel 14,98,100,105
Sanson, Nicolas 14,73,111
Sault Ste. Marie see Jesuits
Scurvy 12,55,57,59-60
Seiche 71
Seneca 4,20,23,25-27,34-40,42-43,48, 58-59,72,86-87,90,98-100,115
Simcoe, Eliz. 42,198 & John Graves 87,98
Six Nations see Five Nations
Slaves and Slavery xiv,1,6
Snow Shoes 12,53
Susquehannocks see Andastes

Talon, Jean xiv,15-16,39,43,47,62-67,79,83-86,96,99,109
Tertian fever… see Malaria
Thoulonnier, Charles 97
Tinaoutoua 1,43-45,47,49,56,58,69, 72,78-79,85, 87,90-94,99-100,108,111,117
Tonty, Henri 100,102
Touguenhas 38-39
Tracey, Alexandre de Prouville 63
Trois Rivières 12,49
Trouvé, Claude 42,83,85,87,97,99,109

Victor, New York 40,98,111,121
Ville Marie…see Montréal

Walker, Iaian C. 100,104-105,117
Wampum 37,43,98,107

Wine at Wintering site 14,51,55,60,100
Wintering Site / Overwintering 50-52 et seq. and
    Appendix A

ABOUT THE AUTHOR

Born at Toronto, Ontario in 1953, John attended the University of Toronto and the University of Windsor. Married to Susie since 1977 he is father of two and a grandfather of recent date. As a member of the Norfolk Historical Society the genesis of this work began in 2012 when Mike McArthur, Barrister planted the seed of the idea in the mind of the author to write about the topic. Thereafter in August of 2013 John presented a lecture on behalf of the Norfolk Historical Society on the Voyage of Dollier and Galinée at Burning Kiln Winery, near to the location where Galinée lost his canoe in the spring of 1670. In 1980 John was called to the Bar as a Member of the Law Society of Upper Canada and for over 30 years served with the Ministry of the Attorney General in the Ontario Crown Prosecution Service as an Assistant Crown Attorney, Crown Attorney and finally as the Assistant Deputy Attorney General and head of the Criminal Law Division for the Province. John and Susie make their home in Norfolk County, not too far from the Wintering Site of Dollier and Galinée.

Ganondagan, Victor New York

www.ingramcontent.com/pod-product-compliance
Lightning Source LLC
Chambersburg PA
CBHW081152090426

42736CB00017B/3286